Ms Moon Presents

# My Moon Mood Journal

Feeling Alchemy and Feminine Embodiment Guide ♥ Menstrual Cycle Journal

Illustrated, Designed, and Authored by Srimati Arya Moon
2nd Edition
©Ms Moon 2018
Do not copy. Do not replicate.
ISBN: 978-1792027833

Ms Moon Publishing
www.msmoon.com

Srimati Arya Moon
Feminine Visionary Artist, Author, and Priestess
www.srimatiaryamoon.com

**Disclaimer:** The information contained in this journal is not intended to treat, prevent, or cure any disease. Before beginning any type of physical exercise or making changes to diet, lifestyle, or psychiatric and/or medical treatment, check with your doctor or therapist.

# My Moon Mood Journal

Love Your Moon

Every woman receives inside herself her own moon to care for. When she loves and nourishes her moon, her moon will blossom and grow into a radiant, glowing full moon, fully reflecting the light of her Feminine Spirit.

—Srimati Arya Moon

# Content Tabs: Cut and Tape

| Alchemy Guide | Menstrual Guide | Month 1 |
| Feeling Practices | Archetype Guide | Month 2 |
| Medicines | Transformation Cycle | Month 3 |

How to Journal

## Write-ins

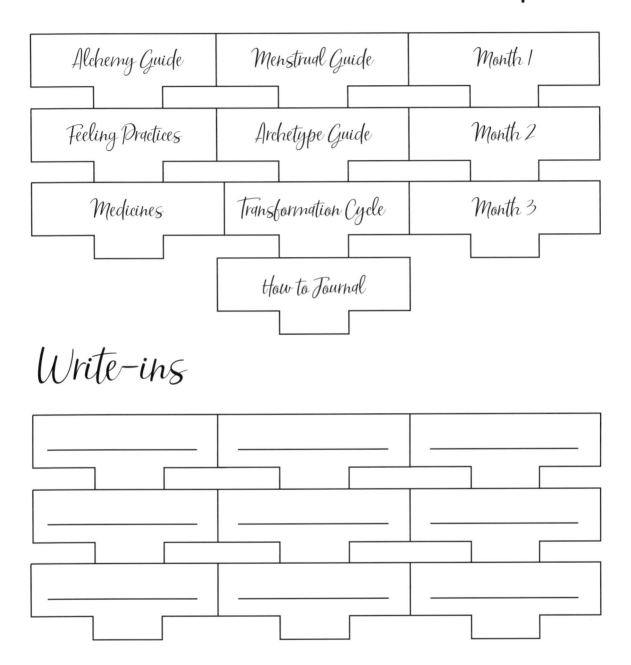

**Instructions**

Cut tabs out and tape them to the side of the correlating page with clear tape. When taping, tape on the front and over the back side of the tab to strengthen the tab.
**Optional:** Before taping, use a highlighter to color code the tabs.

# Letter From Srimati

Welcome Home to your Body.

This journal is your tool and your guide into your cycle, your physical and emotional body, your Feminine Spirit, and your subconscious and unconscious mind. It is a gateway into the deeper aspects of your being and an invitation to return home to your body and cycle to guide you in every aspect of life.

If you are utilizing this journal, it is likely because you heard a call from deep within yourself that whispered to you to find another way:

**Another way to live.
Another way to love.
Another way to come into harmony with yourself—body and nature.**

I truly believe that this path of embracing the mystery and cycles of womanhood is a deeply revolutionary act that will pioneer the way for generations of girls and women to come as we collectively embrace and realize the power of our bodies and their natural rhythms and sensitivity.

Thank you dearly for being right here, right now.

In love, service, and remembrance,

—Srimati

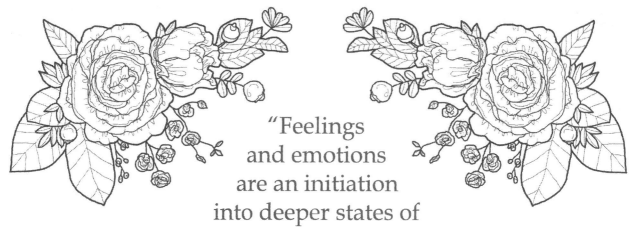

"Feelings and emotions are an initiation into deeper states of awareness. They are a way for us to embody our deepest, purest truth so long as we feel them and allow them to flow."

—Srimati Arya Moon

"Mindfulness means seeing things as they are, without trying to change them. The point is to dissolve our reactions to disturbing emotions, being careful not to reject the emotion itself."

—Tara Bennett-Goleman

# Feminine Embodiment & Feeling Alchemy Guide

As women, we are deeply sensitive, transformational, and cyclical. Honoring our cycles and innate sensitivity and understanding their effect on our feelings from day to day can shift our relationship with ourselves and others. Syncing our awareness to our natural rhythms, transformation, and cycles can lead to greater mind-body harmony; sexual and hormonal health; and a sound mind resilient to anxiety, stress, and fear.

Because of the delicate nature of the female reproductive system and its reliance on different hormones to regulate it, a woman naturally has cycles of feeling and sensitivity shifts throughout the menstrual cycle and at different times and seasons in her life. When we as women dismiss our body and its subtle sensitivity to its environment and inner workings, we devalue our womanhood. That devaluing has impacted our collective female mental and physical health in more ways than one.

This journal seeks to assist women and girls past the age of menstruation in understanding the delicate, cyclical, and transformational nature of their female body by way of somatics and Feminine embodiment—through observation, feeling, embodied presence, and awareness. This journal gives you the tools and guidance in awareness necessary to witness and journal the Feminine transformation cycle, the cycles of the moon and nature, and the rise and fall of feelings in the body based on the principles of Feminine embodiment and feeling alchemy.

This guide offers you a deeper understanding of emotional intelligence and teaches you how to cultivate it. Within 3 months, by dedication to daily journaling, you will be able to develop deeper insight into your body, sensitivity, and feelings, as well as develop greater awareness into the ways your feelings shift and change at different times in your cycle. However, keep in mind that this process of feeling alchemy and Feminine embodiment is a lifelong practice and its fruits are best known after years of self-presence and mindfulness in daily embodied and somatic living. This journal is merely a holistic gateway into a more mature, independent, somatic self-witnessing and listening practice.

## Understanding and Working with Feelings

Feeling is the means through which we, as conscious beings, communicate with our environment, including our bodies. Feeling is what provides us the intelligence we need to both survive and thrive. Feeling is the ability to experience sensation and receive insightful communication from our self and body. Pain, pleasure, urges, desires, and feelings associated with negativity or positivity give us valuable information about our physical and spiritual condition and can help us make decisions based on a combination of instinct, insight, intelligence, and wisdom.

Instinct is a subtle guidance directed by our DNA and mother nature. Instinct is an aspect of our physical body that is based in survival, evolution, and our deep connection to the natural world and mother nature. Our instincts are valuable because they provide us with the intelligence necessary to survive as human beings. They guide us in our basic, intrinsic urges and important needs—our primal nature—and help us know what to do when we enter different stages of development. Instincts guide our rites of passage—into puberty, menstruation, womanhood, partnership, motherhood, menopause, and all the passages dictated by our intrinsic relationship with life.

Insight is much subtler than instinct. It is related to the subtle bodies, our electromagnetic network, and communication with the soul self; the essence of our being that is primordial. Insight and intuition are what allow us to thrive by guiding us on our soul path. Intuition is that feeling and that voice within that guides us in every moment, teaching and showing us how to cultivate our joy and wisdom and connect to our truth, our insight. Insight is the permeation of our essence, Spirit, and wisdom and is what guides our intuition.

Each of us has a need to be connected to both our instinctual self and our insightful self. One grounds us, keeps us safe and provided for in all the ways important to our survival and space of belonging in the world—with our families and groups of identity—and the other gives us guidance, presence, and connection to our subtle self for deep soul satisfaction. The combination of satisfying both our human self and soul self in an integral and wholesome way is what leads to a happy, healthy, and fulfilled life.

Feeling is the medium through which these facets of our self are communicated to our conscious mind. It is the stimulus that sparks our desires and prompts us into action. We need feeling to experience desire and we need desire to take action in any direction, whether that action is toward Spirit or the material.

## Developing Emotional Intelligence

Emotional intelligence is the consciousness of feeling. Developing emotional intelligence is the first step in both understanding feeling and in deepening one's ability to feel. True understanding is to know without reasoning and is a type of wisdom; it is a part of you that you both know and feel. This understanding is about staying deeply present with one's feelings and allowing for a subtle communication to occur. It is the application of opening to receive a deep inner knowing that can only be perceived in a space of humility and surrender—where the mind becomes a conscious and still space for feeling and presence. This type of knowing is called gnosis. The mind's role is to observe, allow, and follow the intelligence of the body so that the gnosis can be known.

## Communicating Feelings Vulnerably

Another aspect of emotional intelligence is vulnerable communication. Vulnerable communication allows you to communicate your feelings and desires to others without defensiveness. You will know when you have developed emotional intelligence when you can vulnerably express your feelings and emotions with an ease and grace that comes naturally; when there is no fight with what you feel or how you express it. As you practice this, keep in mind the process of developing emotional awareness and vulnerability may bring up a lot of resistance and struggle in the beginning, which is a perfectly natural part of the process.

A valuable part of this journal is that by writing out your feelings, emotions, thoughts, and stories, you begin to understand how to communicate them more vulnerably and naturally. Often the struggle is that we in the West are socialized to either repress our feelings or intellectualize and express them without first truly feeling and listening to them. This can distort our ability to vulnerably communicate with others. If we can't first get clear with ourselves, it will be difficult to clearly express ourselves openly to others.

Western models of teaching encourage us to process our feelings by going into our mind — judgment and thought — where we tend to build up identities and stories that reinforce societal programming and our more undesirable moods and emotional patterns. The result is often dissociation or disembodiment and the need for healing work and years of talk therapy. Somatic models, such as yoga, that teach self-awareness and self-presence result in more vulnerability, depth, insight, maturity, gentleness, and flow in how one handles their being and emotions.

## Understanding Internal Programming

Each and every one of us is conditioned by both society and our environment with internal programming and stored memory. Your brain, nervous system, and body are a biological super computer. The brain collects, processes, and stores information and the body possesses its own intelligence and memory via the nervous system, which is an extension of the brain.

Because of this, emotions can get stored in the body within various tissues and organs. Moments of extreme stress and trauma, if not processed from a conscious space of resiliency and safety, can be internally suppressed and held within the body. Much of what I refer to as somatic witnessing is about resolving these emotions by seeing these places within the body — where the body lacks a deep sense of safety due to repressed emotions and/or prolonged periods of stress and trauma.

Stress and trauma can change the nervous system and result in nervous system dysfunction. In psychology, this is known as dysregulation. A recent study by Cambridge University revealed that women are twice as likely to experience prolonged states of stress as men, with one study showing that women were 8 times more likely to experience stress, with the 35 and younger age group being disproportionately affected. Many young women and girls are walking around in states of dysregulation and have no idea what to do about it.

Our moods impact our physical health. High amounts of stress tend to accompany GI tract issues, and trauma related dysregulation can cause illness to manifest in the body. Epigenetics is one such field that is revealing the intimate connection between our environment and genetic expression that encompasses our health and wellness, and can impact generations of women.

There are many techniques to address this state of nervous system dysfunction by emotional/trauma release that involve working with somatic and internal witnessing, which I will discuss in a later section. In order to really understand these processes, it is important to first understand how the body and mind process experiences.

## Moods, Beliefs, Judgments, and Stories

There is a profound connection between the body-mind. The brain is connected to the super highway of the nervous system, which has branches that are woven into every part of the body. The body and the mind are intimately connected in union with cycles of feelings and moods informing upon the body via the sympathetic and parasympathetic nervous system.

A mood is what happens when we allow our feelings to become us. It is an emotional theme that overtakes our sense of being and presence—our identity—for a long time. Instead of saying "I feel", it is often expressed as "I am".

**Example: "I am depressed."**

A mood can affect us based on several factors—our mental and physical health, our attachments, how our thoughts stimulate our feelings, our ability to hold a mood, and how a mood interacts with our nervous system, beliefs, internally held emotions, and environment. These factors create a cycle of feeling and emotions that can perpetuate beliefs and self-identity and can wire our nervous system to be constantly in the fight or flight response (dysregulation).

A belief is when we combine our emotions and feelings with a set of rules to create identities through judgment and story.

**Examples: "I'm anti-sugar. I don't eat sugar. Eating sugar is bad and will make you sick."**

**"I am a sugar-lover. I eat sugar and love sweets. Sugar is good and if you eat sugar with love and gratitude, you will be healthy."**

There have been many studies and historical recordings that reveal just how much our beliefs can affect our body. Psychosomatic phenomena is when the mind's belief or experience leads to a reaction in the body, such that the body is greatly affected. The placebo effect is one such example of psychosomatic phenomena. If indeed a person were to deeply believe sugar was good for them, there would be a higher probability that the consumption of sugar would be well tolerated by their body and even improve one's health. Ironically, the placebo effect is named after the phenomena of giving a sugar pill to a patient with the patient believing they are receiving medication. There is a marked phenomena that occurs where the patient believes the sugar pill has a certain effect in the body that ends up resulting in measurable physical changes.

A judgment is very similar to a belief. It is a conclusion based on a mix of facts, opinions, and reactions.

**Example: "Because he dropped my bag of groceries, he is clumsy."**

Stories are self-narratives of beliefs and thoughts mixed with facts and observations informed on by our underlying beliefs and identities. They are narratives that we tell ourselves about our experiences and understandings of life.

**Example: "I can't believe she said that! She is clearly unhappy with herself and hates me because I remind her of what she doesn't have."**

Our experiences and our self-narratives are what create programs in our body and mind. In yogic philosophy, these programs are called samskaras, and are essentially the energetic (electromagnetic and subtle) wiring of our habitual ways of thinking, feeling, and acting.

All of us engage in habitual ways of thinking, feeling, and acting that are based upon underlying programs of belief and self-identity. While these beliefs serve us in many ways, they cause us harm when they interfere with our joy, relationships, and satisfaction in life or when they contribute to prolonged stress. They are especially harmful when they deceive us into pathologizing, judging, and bullying ourselves and others.

Part of the goal of yoga and journey work is to rewire the mind, body, and energy field to liberate the individual from these samskaras, or programs. Yoga is a type of somatic movement that helps to unlock emotional patterns and rewire the nervous system, and is especially helpful for those suffering with dysregulation. Yoga is not just about doing asanas (postures), but about deepening one's awareness and coming into union with the self—body, mind, and spirit. The techniques taught in yoga can be integrated into any movement, whether it be brushing your teeth or eating your food.

Journey work involves going within one's energy field to remove any harmful beliefs, entities, or traumas and balance out the field of an individual, protecting the individual's sovereignty and sense of self. This powerful type of therapy is effective in healing trauma and can make vast strides in one's mental health and sense of selfhood in short periods of time.

In this journal, you will be utilizing self-witnessing and awareness techniques, such as those found in yoga and journey work, to engage in somatic practice. The goal is to witness the body, its internal movement, and its experience to begin to develop communication and union with the body and its subtle fields. This journal gives you the tools to guide you in feeling into your body and in witnessing the stories and thoughts that naturally emerge as you do. Witnessing these stories and thoughts can give you insight into the way your feelings can be triggered by your underlying beliefs and identities and can assist you in re-patterning your mind where it is desirable to do so.

# How to Work with Your Feelings and Develop Deeper Somatic Awareness

In this guide, I present to you two models of working with feelings and emotions to help you transform your experience with the feeling/thought process altogether, so you can shape your destiny and take command of your experience in life.

## Feelings/Emotions: The Clinical Way

The clinical model in psychology teaches us that feelings are subconscious thoughts we have about our emotions, whereas our emotions are the physical phenomena of what we feel and its body expression, caused by an inner or outer stimulus.

**Sensation>Emotion>Feeling is the cycle that we repeat.**

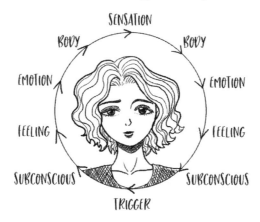

This model explains that the act of dwelling on and creating stories around our feelings can trigger even more sensations in the body, which leads to the cycle repeating itself. Because of this cycle, what one thinks about feeling can train their body to feel sensations it might not usually feel. Thinking becomes a catalyst and a stimulus for feeling.

**Example: The first time I experience being in a high place, I get an uncomfortable, dizzy sensation. I create a story about this experience and identify with "I am afraid of heights". As a result of this belief, the next time I am climbing a ladder, I experience intense sensations that cause me to be triggered – to react. This experience solidifies the belief into my identity: "I am extremely afraid of heights".**

In this model, to say "I feel" has more than one meaning. The subconscious process of thinking and judging is labeled "feeling" due to its association with feeling. Through this approach, it is easy to confuse "to feel" with "feelings as judgments". This may unknowingly elevate our judgments above the actual sensations we experience, and in the process cause us to crystallize those stories and beliefs into our identity. The philosophy "I feel therefore I Am" can become distorted as "I am what I feel".

There are certain aspects of this model that are useful from the lens of Feeling Alchemy.

# Feeling Alchemy

Feeling Alchemy tells us feelings are the sensations and movements we experience that occur in our body in reaction to an external or internal stimulus/cause—including our reactions to our thoughts.

**Example: I am feeling a pressure expanding in the chest, at the same time I feel my eyes dampening and welling with water.**

The emotion, on the other hand, is a process of expressing those feelings by body expression (such as crying or laughing) or by translating them into language and speaking them. The emotion is usually expressed by speaking with the terminology "I feel" or "feeling".

**Examples: I feel sad.**
**I have a strange, uneasy feeling.**

If we pay close attention to what we are saying, it looks like this:

**I recognize the feelings in my body to be sadness.**
**The feeling in my body is unknown to me and causes me to have feelings of anxiousness.**

When we speak of our emotions, we are using a word to describe a series of body sensations—feelings—that we categorize under the umbrella of that word. Sadness may have ten or more sensations and expressions associated with it, but attempting to describe all of those sensations may be difficult or inconvenient. So we call it an emotion—sadness—to simplify our experience.

Feeling alchemy informs us of the need to bring our awareness to the body and allow our emotions and body expressions in a space of internal awareness of movement, perception, and sensation. Rather than going straight to "I feel sad", we allow ourselves to feel every sensation of the emotion by bringing our awareness to the body and its spectrum of feelings. We also allow ourselves the freedom of body expression; if we feel the urge to, we cry, we laugh, we move, we dance, we create art, we make noise. Rather than avoiding the feelings, minimizing them with basic descriptions, and blending them into our thoughts, we truly feel and internally process what we feel in a space of acceptance. We feel and allow the feelings and emotions to flow, intuiting, in connection to our insight, the desired movement of the body in total awareness. And we allow the received gnosis, the awareness, to flow from there.

While we don't use this expression as an excuse to mistreat, dump on, or manipulate others, we don't deny, story, or judge what we feel or the emotions associated with feeling. We take ownership without crystallizing our feelings into our identity. Instead, we stay centered in acceptance for the colorful array of feelings that rise and fall. With time and applied practice, this complete acceptance of feeling transforms and dissolves negative reactions to feeling and helps us center our thoughts on our internal well-being.

This natural, alchemical process eventually dissolves the cycle of negative thought associated with feeling and can help us to work out our fears, frustrations, and anger simply by allowing the process of feeling to exist and work as it is meant to.

The alchemy of feeling—allowing ourselves to truly feel into the sensations of our body, fully connected, integral, and knowing all is well—is what allows us to fully witness, know, communicate with, and accept ourselves. It helps us unstory and unlayer beliefs that harm us. It enables us to take control of the way we relate to our feelings and environment. It is a pathway of absolute personal responsibility.

## Communicating with Self Through Descriptive Observation

As stated in this guide, one of the reasons it is so important to distinguish between thought and feeling is because our bodies communicate to us through feeling. If we are too caught in the loop of thinky-thoughts, we won't be able to hold the awareness necessary to truly listen. Concentrating on the body and holding our presence there helps us to deepen our awareness of self and still the cycle of thought.

Curious and keen observation is the action of awareness. Instead of using judgments to describe what is happening, we observe our experience and move out of the thinking mind. A way of practicing this observation is to narrate it to ourselves as descriptively as possible without creating judgments around those observations.

> **Example: "I am sad and crying. This is terrible! I'm terrible!"**
>
> **Becomes: "A wave is collapsing in my lungs. My eyes are welling with tears and a lump is forming in my throat. A vibration of sound is emerging from my throat and pain and discomfort are billowing up in my neck and lungs."**

Now that you've stilled your mind and noticed this, what else is happening? What sights, smells, textures, tastes, sounds, and memories emerge? What is your body communicating to you? There are a plethora of ways to explore our bodies and their subtle and not-so-subtle ways of communicating with us. You might recall a song lyric or visualize a texture. A memory may pop up or you may receive an internal awareness about yourself that provides you with a deep, personal breakthrough.

## Becoming a Trustworthy/Stable Consciousness for Feeling Alchemy

Just as important as it is to feel your feelings, it is equally important to recognize when a feeling is worthy of being felt, versus when a feeling has gotten so out of hand that the mind destabilizes and the emotional state suffers.

It is important to learn how to become a stable and trustworthy consciousness for your feelings. This is the difference between being able to handle and hold your feelings and becoming so unstable with them that you cause real harm and damage to those you are in relationship with, including yourself. Some feelings absolutely need to be felt and allowed for your healing and deepening. Other feelings need the opposite medicine—bringing them back down into a stable state and regulating the sympathetic and parasympathetic nervous system. This is especially true with certain psychiatric conditions.

A key part of this is simply feeling into your nervous system and learning to recognize when you are overreacting to a stimulus and driving yourself into a fight or flight response. A dysregulated nervous system is the result of being wired for stress, anxiety, and/or a trauma response (stuck in the trauma cycle). To regulate the nervous system, it is drastically important to learn an artform called resiliency.

Resiliency is what enables a person to experience a great deal of stressful stimuli and remain calm within. Developing resiliency skills will help you calm big, out of control emotions and bring your emotional states into a manageable place. This is a foundation of feeling alchemy and it regulates the nervous system to stay in a state of rest while expanding emotional range. It rewires the nervous system for safety and helps one to get out of the trauma cycle.

To do this, you need to develop deeper awareness into your body, which requires somatic skillsets. Become the witness, the still place within, observing the movements of your body and nervous system. Feel your spine and sympathetic nervous system, where it is connected to your solar plexus and heart region. Here is where most people experience out of control and difficult emotions during fight or flight. Feel these sensations in the body and notice when big feelings show up. What is happening around you? What thoughts are running through your head? How can you take care of yourself in this moment?

**Suggestions:** You can use the breath, a mantra, or movement of the body to bring big emotions back down. The most important thing is getting "out of your head" and into the body.

**Haa breaths:** Take in a deep breath through the nose. Hold for a moment, then exhale through the mouth, letting the sound "haa" vibrate your upper chest. Repeat this breath several times or as long as is needed. You can try other breath work as inspired.

**Mantra/Prayer**: You can recite a mantra, scripture, prayer, or positive song lyric in your mind or out loud for as long as is needed. "Peace" is a particularly powerful recitation.

**Movement:** Walk or gently pace. Move your hips from side to side while breathing. Dance or move intuitively. Stretch and reach your arms up and back. Gently twist your spine.

**Other options:** Take a time-out or communicate with a trusted someone how you are feeling (vulnerable communication) and express what you need to calm down. If need be, leave the situation. Discover other ways to support your nervous system so you are taking care of yourself. This will keep you calm and relaxed, activating your parasympathetic nervous system. Go on nature walks, disengage from screens and social media, engage in wholesome and nourishing connection, and take Epsom salt baths. Meditate and pray, sing and chant God's name, or recite holy prayers. Eat nourishing, balanced meals rich in leafy greens and root vegetables. Spend time rooting and grounding into the earth—walking barefoot on the grass or dirt and sitting on and communing with large rocks. Swim in a river or lake or visit a waterfall or the ocean. Touch and commune with animals, plants, and herbs and let yourself receive their connective essence. Exercise; do yoga, dance, gently spin, or hoola hoop. Rub oils on your skin. Get plenty of rest and drink lots of fresh water. Remove yourself from codependant/abusive dynamics and trauma bonds. Eliminate harmful addictions. Face and integrate your shadow aspects without rejecting them.

I encourage you to deepen into these inquiries with somatics and resiliency skills. They are vital skills to develop in working more deeply with your emotions and stretching yourself to expand your feeling capability range and stability while experiencing triggering events.

## Presence, Awareness, and Somatic Living

Once you know how to safely stabalize your emotional state and nervous system, you are ready to go even deeper in your awareness. Feeling Alchemy is about becoming more present and aware. The deeper you concentrate on your body and feel sensations without attaching to, holding onto, or judging them, the deeper your awareness becomes. The deeper you feel, the more present you become. Think of feeling alchemy as a form of moving meditation that is an exercise of awareness.

Presence is the awareness and feeling of your present being and its identity; your essence, body, and environment. An aspect of presence is the ability to project a sense of ease, poise, grace, love, and self-assurance that can only come with fully integrating and accepting one's entire self. It is when the mind is not distracted by thoughts, judgments, and stories and is instead engrossed in the moment and in its experience of being in that moment.

Embodiment requires presence. The wisdom of Feminine embodiment and presence is an inner knowing that you are well, you are whole, and you are integral just as you are, here and now—every single aspect and version of you. The fruit is an innate transformation of depth and richness that occurs as we apply presence to our experiences and embodied, somatic living.

Somatic living is the practice of internal awareness of the physical body and its movements, sensations, and transformation in space and time. It is also the awareness of the body and self in relationship to the world in general. The focus of somatics is on personal transformation through a deep state of internal awareness of movement from within the body.

Movement essentially entails energy in motion; the breath, the beat of the heart, the movement of sensation, the movement of the body, the rhythm of the body, the rhythm of our environment and the ways our environment and relationships impact and influence our belief systems and self-identity. Somatic living is all about developing deep awareness and engaging in personal transformation by way of awareness, presence, and sensual living; being one with our body and merging the self with our life, essentially marrying the spiritual with the physical world.

Somatics is not just about exercise or even meditation. Somatics encompass every single aspect of life. Any activity can become somatic simply by applying awareness and intention of transformation, or alchemy, to our engagements with our self and the world around us. In this way, everyday activities can be a somatic and embodied practice.

When we apply these awareness techniques to our everyday activities and interactions, we can draw from life such a deep richness, presence, and connection that results in great transformation and the embodiment of our spiritual self. Our greater virtues are brought forth while our more undesirable traits are integrated and merged healthily into our being. Our relationships improve and we find ourselves showing up in different ways and vulnerably asking for what we need from those we are relating with. Feminine embodiment relies on this somatic process to work its magic.

## The Way of Feminine Embodiment

Feminine embodiment is the action of integrating the spiritual self and essence into the body. It isn't about gender identity, but an energetic type of embodiment that is internal in nature. In metaphysics, internal awareness and cultivation is a Feminine principle. For women, this deeply activates and connects us to our womanhood and initiates us into rites of passage that become portals of Feminine self-realization that transcend ideas of gender and social constructs—straight to and from the energetic essence and source of the Feminine Being.

Feeling alchemy and somatic living are an important foundation and tenant in Feminine embodiment. This journal teaches Feminine embodiment in combination with feeling alchemy. Through this modality, we do not elevate either feelings or thoughts, but hold space to understand and respect the seasons of their prevalence. We utilize and experience both somatically, with reverence and awareness into the more subtle aspects of the self and body, and see both as whole and complete aspects of our human condition. We develop resiliency skills and expand our range. We experience our everyday living and life as being deeply spiritual in nature and become aware of how Spirit is one with everything always.

This journal serves you in self-empowerment by providing you the tools to center your being on how you feel, observe your cycles, and witness your story so you can finally take control of the narrative of your life and deepen into Feminine embodiment, transformation, and somatic living. It helps you increase your mindfulness and deepen your ability to feel while being rooted and stable. It provides you with medicine-woman and yogic tools to transform yourself at deeply subtle levels. It also empowers you to notice the patterns in your feelings and emotions based on the cycles of your body and the cycles of nature, which is important in helping you understand the delicate, sensitive, and cyclical nature of your female body.

And so it is that through the gateway of your own body and life, you realize yourself and come into union with all that you are.

# Feeling Practices

# Self Listening Practice

## A Feeling is an Observation of Fact; It is an Awareness of Body Sensations

An opinion is not a feeling. It is a thought. They are different and distinct. A valuable skill to develop is to learn how to talk about mental judgments without confusing them with feelings.

**Exercise: Try this. Read the following sentence and then fill in the prompts.**

<u>I am whole, wise, and well within myself.</u>

I feel: _____

I think: _____

I emote: _____

I intuit: _____

**Language to Consider: What do you Feel? Think? Emote? Intuit? Do you know the distinction?**

Get to know each one of them well. Meditate on each word and allow its wisdom to infuse into your being. Now, try practicing this exercise with outer statements and see what comes up. Journal about your experiences.

## Free Journaling

_____
_____
_____
_____
_____
_____
_____
_____
_____

# Body Scan Exercise

This body scan exercise is a tool to help you become present in your body and assist you in your feelings journaling. Sit in a quiet space and set a timer for 5 minutes. Close your eyes. Bring your awareness into your body and feel into it. Without judging or thinking about those sensations, begin to notice areas in your body that are asking for your attention. Feel the different sensations in your body that arise. Every time you catch your mind going into thought or judgment, bring your awareness back to the sensations in your body. Concentrate on feeling those sensations deeper, deeper, deeper, and ever deeper. Once your timer goes off, write about your experiences.

Practice this feeling exercise throughout the day. The more you practice feeling yourself, the more embodied and present you can be with yourself. A good way to do this is to notice the ways your body is responding to its environment. This will help you notice patterns of feeling that are triggered by certain environmental factors.

# Body Scan Free Journaling

_____
_____
_____
_____
_____
_____
_____
_____
_____
_____
_____
_____
_____
_____
_____
_____
_____
_____
_____

# Journeying Into the Self through Feelings

A useful medicine-woman practice is to journey into the Self through feelings. I call this particular practice "The Feeling Vision Quest". In this journey, you will dive into your feelings and utilize your imagination to paint a picture of what the feeling is telling you. In doing so, you are also calling on yourself to resolve the feeling internally by connecting the feeling to the body and the root cause of the feeling. You communicate with your body and ask your body to show you the vision through visualization, then enter into a flow state where the body is able to subtly paint a picture of what the feeling is telling you through an image or story-representation. You can additionally help to resolve the feeling energetically by visualizing a story representation of the feeling and its resolution.

**The Feeling Vision Quest How-to**

This vision quest reveals a type of gnosis to the practitioner. Gnosis is an internal knowing of the body, where the body communicates its wisdom and understanding to your mind. To experience this, you must enter into a meditative state and feel deeply into your feelings and ask the feeling to share the vision with you. As this happens, your mind will receive information; you may receive imagery, sounds, sights, and smells, a song lyric, or memory. The feeling communicates to you. The feeling may even be in connection to what I refer to as "medicines": other plants, animals, lands, waters, elements, planets, and beings.

Now, ask your body to help you resolve the feeling and show to you a representation of the feeling being resolved. Ask your body if there is anything it would like you to do to support it in releasing and resolving the feeling. Once you receive the vision, journal the vision quest in your book.

**Step by Step Instructions**

- Sit in a quiet space. Using the technique taught in the section "Body Scan Exercise", focus your mind and your awareness on the feeling in your body.
- Ask your body to share the vision with you, as described above.
- Now sit still and silently feel into yourself. Observe and listen to what comes up.
- Once you are finished, write about your experience.

# Feeling Vision Quest Free Journaling

# Menstrual Cycle Phases

There are 4 phases in the menstrual cycle: menstruation, follicular phase, ovulation, and the luteal phase.

**Follicular Phase, Day 1-13**: During the follicular phase, your ovaries prepare an egg for the ovulation phase. A hormone called FSH (follicle stimulating hormone) is secreted by the pituitary gland that stimulates the growth of a small group of your egg cells (follicles). A dominant cell, which contains the ovum, will continue to grow into maturity as it prepares for fertilization. It releases estrogen , which stimulates your uterus to create an inner lining of nourishing tissue and cells called the endometrium.

**What you may experience:**

- Steadiness in mood and energy.
- Increased concentration and focus.
- General wellness or sense of well being.
- More extroverted.

**Ovulation, Day 14 (different for every woman)**: During ovulation, the dominant mature follicle ruptures and releases the egg into the fallopian tube with the help of the fimbriae and its cilia, which are located at the end of the fallopian tube near the ovaries. This prepares the egg for fertilization. The released egg will stay in the fallopian tube for about 24 hours as it waits to be fertilized.

**What you may experience:**

- Increased basal body temperature by a ½ degree.
- Increased energy and changes in libido.
- More extroverted.
- A heightened sense of smell and other senses.
- Changes in cervical mucus.
- Light spotting.
- Fertility Awareness Method (FAM) can help you determine ovulation.

**Luteal Phase, Day 15-28 and Beyond (some extend to 32 days or longer)**: The ruptured follicle transforms into a structure called the corpus luteum that releases progesterone. The corpus luteum and egg enter the uterus. If the egg was never fertilized, the corpus luteum dissolves and the hormones it secretes eventually run out, causing the endometrium to shed and expel.

**What you may experience:**

**Part 1: Estrogen has peaked and progesterone increases.**

- You may feel more relaxed, calm, and serene.

**Part 2: Progesterone and estrogen drop significantly.**

- Increased sensitivity and feeling—irritability and emotional sensitivity.
- Decrease in energy.
- More introverted.

**Drop in hormones may induce PMS (pre-menstrual symptoms). PMS Symptoms include:**

- Tiredness and mood swings.
- Sudden depression or anxiety.
- Light abdominal cramping, signaling the start of menses.
- Tenderness in breasts, lower back, pelvis, and legs.
- Changes in appetite.
- Acne/skin changes.

**Menstruation, Day 1-7 (maybe shorter or longer, depending on the woman):** Menstruation is the first day of your cycle. During the menstrual phase of your cycle, your uterus sheds the endometrium through the vagina.

**What you may experience:**

- Blood loss of 10 ml to 80 ml; severe bleeding more than 80 ml is known as menorrhagia.
- Abdominal cramps, which are caused by a hormonal secretion that causes the contraction of the uterus to expel the endometrium; this cramping is known as dysmenorrhea.
- Tender back, pelvis, and thighs.
- Tiredness and mood swings brought on by physical discomfort.
- More introverted.
- Highly sensitive.

# Cycle Transformation, Cycle Seasons, and Cycle Archetypes

Cycling women are moving through a transformational cycle that takes them into 5 different archetypes, depending on her cycle phase and what season she is in. This transformational cycle takes her through a birthing and dying process. Her dying occurs at the end of each cycle and she is rebirthed in her follicular phase after she moves through her bleeding. Understanding these facets is another way to help know how to best support yourself and utilize your energy at different points in your cycle. These seasons and moon phases can also be associated with the cycles of the moon—with the first day of menstruation being your New Moon and ovulation being your Full Moon. This is why many refer to their menstrual period as their "moontime".

# Cycle Moon Phases

During the cycling years of a woman's life, she is synced up to a moon rhythm that is internal rather than external. This means that rather than being guided by the lunar moon for guidance in her life, she will follow her internal moon and rhythm, which may differ from that of the lunar moon cycle. In my womb lineage, we refer to the internal cycle as a moon cycle, the difference is that this cycle is unique for each woman and often has nothing to do with what the lunar moon is doing, although some women do cycle with the New Moon and have rhythms synced up to the lunar cycle.

While a faucet of this journal is observing and journaling the lunar moon cycle and Zodiac, understand that this is more for the sake of observation and connecting to and witnessing nature's rhythms. It is a tool added for those women who are not experiencing a bleeding cycle or for whom tracking the lunar moon is important for their spiritual observances.

The following sections illustrates the transformation cycle and these cycle seasons, cycle moon phases, and the associated guiding archetypes. Have fun coloring these pages in as you learn about the mysteries of your moontime. Use the "Notes" section on the back of each page to journal important information about this time of your cycle. Consider what sort of activities you'd like to do, what type of foods and supplements you'd like to eat, and how you can organize your time, Feminine embodiment/somatic movement, and attention for this particular phase.

# Waxing Moon Cycle Notes

## Spring | Waxing Moon

**Phase:** After Menses into the Follicular Phase

**Archetype:** Maiden / Child

**Description:** You are budding as your body prepares for ovulation.

**Action:** This is a powerful time to open up your receptivity to life, take leaps of faith, pursue education, have fun and be active, pursue goals, and draw your desires toward you. Eat nourishing foods that feed healthy hormones and support the liver and kidneys.

**Qualities:** Innocent, playful, moving, active, expanding, growing, belief, faith, extroverted, explorative, manifesting, creative, imaginative, and learning.

# Full Moon Cycle Notes

## Summer | Full Moon

**Phase:** Ovulation

**Archetype:** Mother/Lover

**Description:** In the summer, you are at your most fertile, social, energetic, and radiant. Your basal body temperature rises.

**Action:** This is a peak time for manifestation, creativity, and being more outward with your work and social life. Spend this time socializing, organizing outwardly, and actualizing plans. Eat nourishing foods and herbs that support your fertility.

**Qualities:** Energetic, confident, active, expanding, extroverted, adventurous, passionate, penetrative, creative, fertile, actualizing, and pleasureful.

# Waning Moon Cycle Notes

## P1-Harvest | P2-Autumn | Waning Moon

**Phase:** The Luteal Phase (Two Parts)

**Archetype:** Part 1 Healer. Part 2 Wild Woman

**Description:** You are receding back into yourself and your sensitivity drastically increases as your progesterone and estrogen levels peak and then fall.

**Action:** This is a powerful time for healing, cleansing, and beginning to prepare yourself to release and shed. Soften into yourself as you dip into deeper emotions, sensitivity, and shadow. Tap into your instincts and intuition to cultivate inner transformation. Connect with nature and play with plants and herbs. Eat foods that nourish the liver and keep blood sugar levels stable.

**Qualities:** Mature, calm, contracting, introverted, deep, present, aware, critical, feeling, and sensitive.

# New Moon Cycle Notes

Winter | New Moon

**Phase:** Menstrual Phase

**Archetype:** Crone-Priestess

**Description:** You are releasing and shedding physically, emotionally, and energetically.

**Action:** You are at your most sensitive. Engage in activities such as journaling, ritual, meditation, and prayer. Spend time resting. Observe and witness unseen facets of yourself and bring them into the light for healing and integration. This is a time to release and let go of all that no longer serves you. Eat grounding foods like root vegetables and mineral rich foods.

**Qualities:** Introspective, wise, integrative, inert, inactive, contracting, introverted, prayerful, aware, perceptive, present, releasing, bleeding, cleansing, deep, quiet, restful, and sensitive.

# Working with Medicines

In my spiritual lineage, medicines are the potency contained in the essence of a being or element. All things created contain elements and have composition. Their "isness" is what determines their purpose and function. This "isness" holds wisdom and gnosis and is the revealer of the medicine.

While working with the menstrual cycle and cycle witnessing, understanding how to be attuned to gnosis and its revealed medicines is incredibly powerful. In the provided journaling pages and "The Wheel of Transformation", these pages are designed for a woman to tap into the medicines that desire to work with her by the revelation of themes, feelings and awarenesses.

**How to Work with Medicines**

By practicing the body scan exercise in this journal, you will be able to feel into your body and listen for subtle communication. Allow your connection to Spirit and God to guide your revelation. Feel into this connection and ask, "What medicines desire to work with me today?" While there are many medicines to work with, the answer may simply be a single medicine to focus on in a given day, even if you do other activities and make more than one connection. Pay attention to specifics or interactions that stand out above the rest and feel especially medicinal and revelatory.

Now pay attention to what comes up and the feelings in your body when you work with these medicines. You may be guided to immerse yourself in water, earth, or grass. You may be guided to sing a song or recite scripture. Pay attention to your cycle and the medicines of your hormones and where you are at in the cycle. This will help you to receive the wisdom of the medicines and how they are activating you. As you begin to work with these medicines, journal on the awarenesses that arise or simply allow what is being experienced to reach into you and transform you. Because there can be so much all at once, it may not be possible to write everything down, but simply allow the experience, wisdom, and healing to transform you.

On the back of the Kuan Yin color page, you can write down a list of medicines that come to mind that have been working with and for you. Use the list on the next page to get an idea about the medicines that may be present in your life. A medicine is active in your life when you can feel its subtle influence activating you and initiating you more deeply into your self.

# Medicines Active in My Life

# Examples of Medicines Helpful for Cycle Witnessing:

In the Body

> **Hormones:** Estrogen class hormones, progesterone, FSH, cortisol, oxytocin, melatonin, dopamine, testosterone, prolactin, and insulin are all examples of hormones that effect women's cycles, stress response, and sexuality. The body produces many more hormones. If you would like to dive deeper into understanding these hormones, I recommend researching a list of human hormones and their function.
>
> **Autonomic Nervous System — Parasympathetic and Sympathetic Nervous System:** The Sympathetic nervous system is the nervous system responsible for your "fight or flight" responses in times of emergencies. It controls the body's responses to stress, injuries, or perceived threats. When activated, functions not critical to survival shut down. The Parasympathetic nervous system is the nervous system responsible for your "rest and digest" responses in times of non-emergencies. Its job is to counterbalance; it restores the body to a state of calm.
>
> **Female Body and Womb:** Breasts, uterus, uterine lining, fallopian tubes, follicles, egg, vagina, clitoris, vulva.
>
> **Body Functions:** Digestion, breathing, heartbeat. Engaging the senses; touch, taste, smell, sound, sight.

**Nature:** Sky, air, earth, waters, mountains, valleys. Plants, flowers, trees, herbs, roots, fruits, vegetables. Animals, birds, insects, fish of all variety. Rocks, crystals, minerals, metals, soil, clay, red earth. Cosmos, planets, stars, constellations, sun.

**Food:** All foods and liquids, supplements, herbals, pharmacology.

**Elements:** Earth, fire, wind, water, and ether.

**Beings:** Angels, God Family, Ancestors, Saints, Sages.

**People:** Communing and connecting with parents, siblings, aunts, uncles, cousins, grandparents, spouse/partner, children, friends, healers, mentors, teachers, strangers.

**Sound:** Words, vocalizations, music, mantra, recitations, reading aloud, speaking aloud, listening to the sounds of nature or the rhythms of the Mother Earth and Father Sky.

**Breath and Vibration:** Breathing practices and rhythm, drumming, vibration instruments.

**Movement/Activities:** Exercise, dance, yoga, walking, cleaning, hand gestures, yoni steaming, eating with friends, working with plants, making art, writing, playing, eros.

# The Transformation Cycle

Every cycle, a woman is moving through transformation. This transformation is cosmological in nature and mirrors our matriarchal origin—the cosmic womb, the spiral. During our Follicular-Ovulating phases, we are moving through an outward spiral. Our energy becomes externally directed. During our Luteal-Menstrual phase, we move through an inward spiral. Our energy becomes internally directed.

Every woman will notice themes emerging with each cycle for her to work and transform with. In this journal, I have included a womb wheel for each cycle (three total) for women to work with called "The Wheel of Transformation". This wheel incorporates the transformation cycle, working with transformational themes that activate initiation and rites of passage. If a woman is partnered, it is a good idea for her to share these themes with her partner, as it is extremely likely her partner is being influenced by them.

## The Wheel of Transformation

**Rebirth | Follicular**
The whole self is now cohesive and reborn from the previous cycle. The themes you received are activated and come to the surface of your awareness to be worked with and explored. You receive the nourishing medicines of the womb that build up and nourish the lining of the womb.

**Themes Take Root:** The transformational themes that were received by you during your previous menses take root within you.
**Themes Budding:** The themes begin to bud and are emerging from the ground of your consciousness, expanding outward.
**Themes Growing:** The themes grow as you move more outward in the spiral. The nourishing medicines of the womb reach the themes and activate them into a nourishing expansion.

**Maturing | Ovulation**
The self is entering into a heightened time of eros for implantation. The theme's fertility and expression is revealed to you. Now is the time to ask yourself what is the essence and potency of this cycle's themes? What is the creative potential they contain? How are they expressing in me? How can I play passionately with them?

**Themes Blossom:** The themes now begin to blossom. They reveal themselves more fully, joyfully, and pleasurefully.
**Themes Touch Eros:** The themes make contact with love and desire. This invites you into play as your sexual energy is activated and you begin to explore your desires with them.
**Themes Pollinated:** The themes are pollinated by your contact with love and eros. They now contain deeper, richer potency and enter a maturation stage. The theme's expression is revealed through your self-expression and creativity.

## Culminating | Luteal

During this time, you are playing with the nourisher archetype. The unfertilized egg descends into the womb and your feel-good hormones increase. The themes you are working with ripen and fruit. You receive the fruits of the themes and use them to nourish and heal yourself.

**Themes Fruiting:** The themes begin to fruit.
**Themes Ripen:** As the themes fruit, they begin to ripen. This ripening takes you into deeper awareness and reveals more mature insight.
**Themes Harvested:** The theme's fruit is harvested, and the fruit nourishes the body and self. The medicines of the womb reach, activate, and nourish you. You are existing with these themes in a place of deep fulfillment as they nourish you inside and out. This fruit becomes a medicine and you receive healing, activation, and deeper initiation.

## Dying | Late Luteal

The releasing medicine of the womb activates. As the unfertilized egg dissolves, hormones drop and this becomes a medicine that roots out what is needed to be released this cycle. It signals the body to shed the lining of the womb, but it also becomes a medicine that signals the themes you are working with to root out the shadow for integration and release.

**Medicine Reaches Themes:** The womb's medicine makes contact with this cycle's themes.
**Shadow is Revealed:** You now may experience difficult emotions surrounding this cycle's themes. You are more aware of all of the things that are bothering you and feel more critical and sensitive.
**Preparation for Release:** You can feel your body and self ready to release and let go of what is no longer serving you so you can integrate the themes and their lessons within your being.

## Death | Menstruation

It is time to die. Your old self is no more and you are now shedding and releasing. You receive aspects of yourself that were not available to you before. You integrate the full cycle and go into a deep, receptive, restful state.

**Releasing and Shedding:** Your body releases the lining of the womb, along with anything within the psyche that is ready to be released with the full culmination of the transformational cycle.
**Soul Pieces Retrieved—Plants Seeds:** You receive pieces of yourself that were lost to you. Those pieces come back home to the self to prepare for rebirth. You receive the seeds for the next transformation cycle, and they are planted within your consciousness.
**Integrate the Cycle—Incubation:** The cycle is integrated. Lessons and shadow aspects are integrated. What no longer serves has been released. You enter a state of wholeness and incubation as your body begins the birthing process.

**Rebirth: A New Cycle Begins.**

# How-to: The Wheel of Transformation

**The Wheel of Transformation will help you deepen into your transformation cycle. This journal provides you with three wheels, one for each cycle you move through.**

**How to Fill it Out**: In each of the five sections, using the prompts on the outer edge of the wheel, you will write in each section the themes as they relate to their correlating cycle transitions. Use the sample page to see what this looks like.

**Tip:** When filling out the Wheel of Transformation, use the "Notes" section on the adjacent page to write in any extra insights you have about your transformation cycle.

**Spring:** What themes are emerging from your consciousness? How are they budding? How are they growing? Can you feel any medicines activating them? Feel the medicines of the womb and the medicines of nature and how they interact with these themes.

**Summer:** What is the essence and potency of this cycle's themes? What is the creative potential they contain? How are they expressing in you? How can you play passionately with them? What desires are emerging with them?

**Harvest:** What are the fruits of this cycle's themes? How are they nourishing you and healing you? How are they activating and initiating you?

**Autumn:** What are the theme's shadows within you? Where are you experiencing corruption with these themes? What desires to be released, healed, and integrated?

**Winter:** What is being released? What parts of you have been returned? What are you receiving? What are you integrating?

**A Note About Partners and Family Members:**

I encourage women to share this information with their family members, especially their partners. This will help the household to become more womb-guided. What this means is that the needs of the womb-bodied are being honored and what is emerging through her is being valued within the home. This transformation cycle is incredibly valuable and can be a tremendous asset to a family when it is honored and shown reverence. When mothers embody the knowledge, they transmit it to their daughters through their example. When fathers and husbands honor the womb, daughters and sons receive this example and will more deeply honor themselves and women as a result. Coming into harmony with these teachings can greatly reduce anxiety and stress in the home and help a family to align to a more harmonious, cosmic rhythm that creates more peace and love in the home.

# Sample Page

# Wheel of Transformation

## WINTER | NEW MOON
*Outer ring:* Soul Pieces Returned: Plant Seeds · Integrate Last Cycle: Incubation · Rebirth Follicular · Shedding/Releasing · Death Menstruation

While bleeding, I felt myself releasing so much of my fear and distrust for my body and its mechanisms. I received a part of myself back to me called "home root." Home Root is the part of me that safe and rooted no matter where she is. I lost her when I was a child and moved so much I didn't trust it to be safe.

## SPRING | WAXING MOON
*Outer ring:* Themes Take Root · Themes Budding · Themes Growing · Maturation Fertility/Ovulation

My body is my home. I am safe in my body. Pain does not mean illness. My nervous system is beginning to activate as I somatically feel into these themes budding and growing. I can feel my hormones nourish and build my womb up. My body is responding to my repatterning. I am well.

## SUMMER | FULL MOON
*Outer ring:* Themes Blossom · Touch Eros · Themes Pollinated

The essence of these themes is innate inner wellness. These themes show me I have the ability to play inside my body with sensation and experiencing. I can repattern myself to feel safe even if I have a point in my body as if it is a problem. I want to see my body as if it is pristine.

## HARVEST | WANING MOON
*Outer ring:* Culminating Wheat · Egg Releases Medicine · Themes Fruit · Fruit Harvested · Themes Ripen Heal/Nourish

The fruits of this cycle's themes are cultivating an innate wellness, deeper relationship with my body and deeper trust in my body. They are nourishing me by teaching me deep wholesome body connection. They heal my relationship with my body. I am being more deeply initiated into my body, health, and state of wellness.

## AUTUMN | WANING MOON
*Outer ring:* Dying Wheat Womb Medicine Late Luteal Peaches Themes · Shadow Revealed · Preparation for Release

I am realizing how much I lack trust in myself. Any little pain scares me especially with pain. I have a serious disease. I don't want to live without this fear really left my body, anxiety has taken over. I feel this conniption in my energy field where fear and distrust live. I wish to release this fear, root, and integrate.

# How to Journal

## Mirrored Calendar System

The calendar system is designed to help you witness and record your cycle and the cycle of the moon side by side a planning calendar.

### The Left Calendar: Moon Mapping Calendar

The left calendar is a moon mapping calendar for mapping your inner moon, the lunar moon, and moon zodiac. In the top box write in the month, year, and season. In the upper left corner of each date box, write in the dates for the month. Next, in the lower right-hand corner, write in your cycle day. The first day of your cycle is the first day of menstruation. In the circle above this box, fill in the size and shape of the moon on that day (refer to a lunar calendar). You can also add other information here, such as the moon zodiac and your fertility status.

### The Right Calendar: Monthly Intuitive Desire Calendar for Deepening Resiliency

This calendar is a mirror of your other calendar and is about cultivating resiliency. Fill in the same information: month, year, season, and number your dates. Next, fill in desired activities that support where you are at in your cycle according to the information on the left calendar.

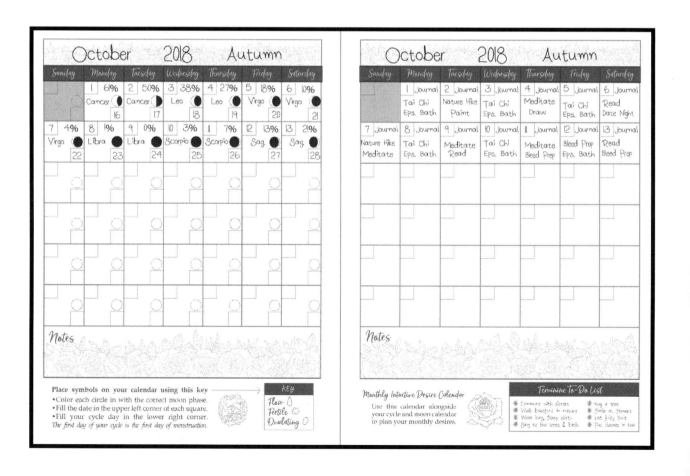

# How to Use for Non-bleeding Women

If you are not bleeding because you are post-menopausal, because of hysterectomy, or other instances where there is no menstrual cycle, it is still possible to use this journal. Simply use the lunar moon in the sky as a guide instead of your inner moon cycle.

Each stage of the cycle will correlate to where the moon is at in its cycle:

**New Moon**-Releasing "bleeding", correlates to menstruation.
**Waxing Moon**-Growing "expanding", correlates to follicular phase.
**Full Moon**-Full "fertile", correlates to ovulation.
**Waning Moon**-Shrinking "receding", correlates to luteal phase.

You can use the guide provided in the "Go With the Flow Menstrual Guide" to receive guidance at each moon phase and receive understanding on how to work with the lunar moon. By correlating the moon phases to the menstrual cycle moon phase, season, and archetype, you will connect deeply to the moon mysteries and Feminine Essence even if you are not experiencing ovulation and bleeding cycles.

When filling in the journal prompts and spaces, follow the lunar moon to record your cycle moon phase, cycle season, guiding archetype, and cycle day as pictured below:

---

Date: 05.18.2018     Season: Spring

Day of Week: Friday     Time of Day: Evening ✻ 9pm     Moon Zodiac: Cancer

Moon Phase: Waxing Crescent ☾ 18%     Cycle Moon Phase: Waxing Moon

Cycle Phase: _____     Cycle Season/Archetype: Spring ✻ Maiden     Cycle Day: 5

---

Both the journaling pages and the calendar system will assist you in observing the lunar phases, which makes this journal perfect for both bleeding and non-bleeding women.

# How to Fill in Journal Pages

**Top Section: Fill in the Date, Season, Day of Week, Time of Day**
**Moon Zodiac**: Write in what Zodiac sign the moon is currently in.

**Moon Phase:** Write out the phase of the moon. Then color in the circle with the current shape of the moon.
**Cycle Moon Phase:** Write in the moon phase of your internal moon.

**Cycle Phase**: Write in the cycle phase you are in.
**Cycle Season and Archetype**: Write the cycle season you are in and the archetype associated with it.
**Cycle Day:** Write in your cycle day.

**Fertile, PMS/Cramps, and Flow:** This section helps you assess your cycle and menstrual pain levels. You can learn more about fertility by researching the Fertility Awareness Method. Use this section to record your PMS/menstrual symptoms. In the "Flow" section, fill in the graphic based on the intensity of your blood flow.

**Hours of Sleep:** Write in your hours of sleep from the previous night here.
**Mood:** What do you notice your mood to be today?
**Present Statement:** How do you desire to be present with yourself today?
**Transformation Themes:** What transformation themes are you exploring today?

**Medicines:** What medicines are you working with today?
**I Feel in my Body:** Feeling into your body; what sensations are arising within? Do you feel feelings in connection to any medicines?
**Take note of the body diagram in the left corner.** In this diagram, intuitively draw into the body based on how you feel. You can use the figure as a base to draw around and create a more realistic model of your body, as pictured in the example.

**Environment/Notes:** What is happening in your environment?

**I Feel Emotionally:** What honest emotions are arising in your body?
**I think-Beliefs/Stories/Awarenesses:** What beliefs, stories, and awarenesses are coming up right now?
**I Am Weaving:** How are you weaving your transformation themes into this day and time? With the moon? With the planets? With this time in your cycle? What are you consciously weaving in the tapestry of your life and bringing home?
**I Intuit/Desire:** What is your intuition telling you? What do you desire?

# Sample Page

**Date:** 05 18 2018    🌒    **Season:** Spring

**Day of Week:** Friday    **Time of Day:** Evening ✻ 9pm    **Moon Zodiac:** Cancer

**Moon Phase:** Waxing Crescent & 18% 🌒    **Cycle Moon Phase:** Waning Moon

**Cycle Phase:** Luteal    **Cycle Season/Archetype:** Autumn Wild Woman    **Cycle Day:** 24

**Fertile:** ✿✿✿✿✿ O    **PMS/Cramps:** ✦✦✦✦✦    **Flow:** ○○○○○

**Hours of Sleep:** 9    **Mood:** Calm and relaxed.

**Present Statement:** My Body is my home.

**Transformation Theme:** Gnosis with my body and health, how it is tied to my wellbeing and sense of safety in my body.

**Medicines:** Sky, mountain, sitting in the grass, and reading a book on ancient languages.

**I Feel in my Body:** I feel a dull ache under my left breast. There is a heaviness in my lower digestive tract. I felt a light fluttering in my gut and pleasure in my heart. I feel an expansiveness connected to visualization of the sky. This expansiveness grows within my chest and solar plexus whenever I think about the sky.

**Environment/Notes:** Recently, it has been more difficult to keep my space clean and organized. My room needs cleaning and the laundry needs to be done.

# Sample Page

**I Feel Emotionally:** I feel a bit of stress, but I also feel happy, relaxed, and peaceful in my heart.

**I Think-Beliefs/Stories/Awarenesses:** I think I am still struggling with fear of pain and illness in my body. I notice that I unconsciously tell myself when I feel pain that there must be something wrong with me.

**I Am Weaving:** Themes of wholeness are coming up. I am weaving stories of my wholeness into myself and allowing myself to integrate these shadow aspects that tell me to be afraid of my body.

**I Intuit/Desire:** I desire health, wholeness and wellness and I desire to be more present with my body. My intuition is telling me to trust my body instead of assume there is something wrong with her.

To Your Moon and Back

# Month 1

**Place symbols on your calendar using this key**
- Color each circle in with the correct moon phase.
- Fill the date in the upper left corner of each square.
- Fill your cycle day in the lower right corner.

*The first day of your cycle is the first day of menstruation.*

### KEY
Flow ○
Fertile ✿
Ovulating ○

| Sunday | Monday | Tuesday | Wednesday | Thursday | Friday | Saturday |
|---|---|---|---|---|---|---|
|  |  |  |  |  |  |  |
|  |  |  |  |  |  |  |
|  |  |  |  |  |  |  |
|  |  |  |  |  |  |  |
|  |  |  |  |  |  |  |
|  |  |  |  |  |  |  |

**Notes**

*Monthly Intuitive Desire Calendar*

Use this calendar alongside your cycle and moon calendar to plan your monthly desires.

### Feminine To-Do List

- ❋ Commune with sisters
- ❋ Walk barefoot in nature
- ❋ Wear long, flowy skirts
- ❋ Sing to the trees & birds
- ❋ Hug a tree
- ❋ Smile at flowers
- ❋ Eat juicy fruit
- ❋ Put flowers in hair

# Notes

# Wheel of Transformation

# Notes

Date: _____ Season: _____

Day of Week: _____ Time of Day: _____ Moon Zodiac: _____

Moon Phase: _____ Cycle Moon Phase: _____

Cycle Phase: _____ Cycle Season/Archetype: _____ Cycle Day: _____

Fertile: ✿ ✿ ✿ ✿ ✿ ○     PMS/Cramps: ✦ ✦ ✦ ✦ ✦     Flow: ◯ ◯ ◯ ◯ ◯

Hours of Sleep: _____ Mood: _____

Present Statement: _____
Transformation Theme: _____

Medicines: _____

I Feel in my Body: _____

Environment/Notes: _____

I Feel Emotionally: _____

I Think-Beliefs/Stories/Awarenesses: _____

I Am Weaving: _____

I Intuit/Desire: _____

Date: _____ Season: _____

Day of Week: _____ Time of Day: _____ Moon Zodiac: _____

Moon Phase: _____ Cycle Moon Phase: _____

Cycle Phase: _____ Cycle Season/Archetype: _____ Cycle Day: _____

Fertile: ✿ ✿ ✿ ✿ ✿ ○     PMS/Cramps: ✯ ✯ ✯ ✯ ✯     Flow: ◯ ◯ ◯ ◯ ◯

Hours of Sleep: _____ Mood: _____

Present Statement: _____

Transformation Theme: _____

Medicines: _____
_____
_____

I Feel in my Body: _____
_____
_____
_____
_____
_____
_____
_____

Environment/Notes: _____
_____
_____
_____
_____
_____
_____

I Feel Emotionally: _____

I Think–Beliefs/Stories/Awarenesses: _____

I Am Weaving: _____

I Intuit/Desire: _____

Date: _____  Season: _____

Day of Week: _____  Time of Day: _____  Moon Zodiac: _____

Moon Phase: _____  Cycle Moon Phase: _____

Cycle Phase: _____  Cycle Season/Archetype: _____  Cycle Day: _____

Fertile: ✿ ✿ ✿ ✿ ✿ ○  PMS/Cramps: ☆ ☆ ☆ ☆ ☆  Flow: ◯ ◯ ◯ ◯ ◯

Hours of Sleep: _____  Mood: _____

Present Statement: _____

Transformation Theme: _____

Medicines: _____
_____
_____

I Feel in my Body: _____
_____
_____
_____
_____
_____
_____
_____

Environment/Notes: _____
_____
_____
_____
_____
_____

*I Feel Emotionally:* _____

*I Think—Beliefs/Stories/Awarenesses:* _____

*I Am Weaving:* _____

*I Intuit/Desire:* _____

Date: _____  Season: _____

Day of Week: _____   Time of Day: _____   Moon Zodiac: _____

Moon Phase: _____ ○   Cycle Moon Phase: _____

Cycle Phase: _____   Cycle Season/Archetype: _____   Cycle Day: _____

Fertile: ✽✽✽✽✽ ○   PMS/Cramps: ✯✯✯✯✯   Flow: ◊◊◊◊◊

Hours of Sleep: _____   Mood: _____

Present Statement: _____

Transformation Theme: _____

Medicines: _____
_____
_____

I Feel in my Body: _____
_____
_____
_____
_____
_____
_____
_____

Environment/Notes: _____
_____
_____
_____
_____
_____
_____

*I Feel Emotionally:* _____

*I Think–Beliefs/Stories/Awarenesses:* _____

*I Am Weaving:* _____

*I Intuit/Desire:* _____

Date: _____  Season: _____

Day of Week: _____ Time of Day: _____ Moon Zodiac: _____

Moon Phase: _____ Cycle Moon Phase: _____

Cycle Phase: _____ Cycle Season/Archetype: _____ Cycle Day: _____

Fertile: ✿ ✿ ✿ ✿ ✿ ○   PMS/Cramps: ☆ ☆ ☆ ☆ ☆   Flow: ◊ ◊ ◊ ◊ ◊

Hours of Sleep: _____ Mood: _____

Present Statement: _____

Transformation Theme: _____

Medicines: _____

I Feel in my Body: _____

Environment/Notes: _____

I Feel Emotionally: _____

I Think—Beliefs/Stories/Awarenesses: _____

I Am Weaving: _____

I Intuit/Desire: _____

Date: _____  Season: _____

Day of Week: _____  Time of Day: _____  Moon Zodiac: _____

Moon Phase: _____  Cycle Moon Phase: _____

Cycle Phase: _____  Cycle Season/Archetype: _____  Cycle Day: _____

Fertile: ✿✿✿✿✿ ○  PMS/Cramps: ✯✯✯✯✯  Flow: ○○○○○

Hours of Sleep: _____  Mood: _____

Present Statement: _____

Transformation Theme: _____

Medicines: _____

I Feel in my Body: _____

Environment/Notes: _____

I Feel Emotionally: _____

I Think—Beliefs/Stories/Awarenesses: _____

I Am Weaving: _____

I Intuit/Desire: _____

Date: _____ Season: _____

Day of Week: _____ Time of Day: _____ Moon Zodiac: _____

Moon Phase: _____ Cycle Moon Phase: _____

Cycle Phase: _____ Cycle Season/Archetype: _____ Cycle Day: _____

Fertile: ✿ ✿ ✿ ✿ ✿ ○    PMS/Cramps: ☆ ☆ ☆ ☆ ☆    Flow: ◯ ◯ ◯ ◯ ◯

Hours of Sleep: _____ Mood: _____

Present Statement: _____

Transformation Theme: _____

Medicines: _____

I Feel in my Body: _____

Environment/Notes: _____

I Feel Emotionally: _____

I Think-Beliefs/Stories/Awarenesses: _____

I Am Weaving: _____

I Intuit/Desire: _____

Date: _____  Season: _____

Day of Week: _____  Time of Day: _____  Moon Zodiac: _____

Moon Phase: _____  Cycle Moon Phase: _____

Cycle Phase: _____  Cycle Season/Archetype: _____  Cycle Day: _____

Fertile: ✿ ✿ ✿ ✿ ✿ ○   PMS/Cramps: ✦ ✦ ✦ ✦ ✦   Flow: ○ ○ ○ ○ ○

Hours of Sleep: _____  Mood: _____

Present Statement: _____

Transformation Theme: _____

Medicines: _____

I Feel in my Body: _____

Environment/Notes: _____

I Feel Emotionally: _____
_____
_____

I Think–Beliefs/Stories/Awarenesses: _____
_____
_____
_____
_____
_____
_____
_____
_____
_____
_____
_____
_____
_____

I Am Weaving: _____
_____
_____
_____
_____

I Intuit/Desire: _____
_____
_____
_____
_____

Date: _____  Season: _____

Day of Week: _____  Time of Day: _____  Moon Zodiac: _____

Moon Phase: _____  Cycle Moon Phase: _____

Cycle Phase: _____  Cycle Season/Archetype: _____  Cycle Day: _____

Fertile: ✿ ✿ ✿ ✿ ✿ ○   PMS/Cramps: ✡ ✡ ✡ ✡ ✡   Flow: ◊ ◊ ◊ ◊ ◊

Hours of Sleep: _____  Mood: _____

Present Statement: _____

Transformation Theme: _____

Medicines: _____

I Feel in my Body: _____

Environment/Notes: _____

I Feel Emotionally: _____

I Think-Beliefs/Stories/Awarenesses: _____

I Am Weaving: _____

I Intuit/Desire: _____

Date: _____ Season: _____

Day of Week: _____ Time of Day: _____ Moon Zodiac: _____

Moon Phase: _____ Cycle Moon Phase: _____

Cycle Phase: _____ Cycle Season/Archetype: _____ Cycle Day: _____

Fertile: ✿ ✿ ✿ ✿ ✿ ○    PMS/Cramps: ✰ ✰ ✰ ✰ ✰    Flow: ◊ ◊ ◊ ◊ ◊

Hours of Sleep: _____ Mood: _____

Present Statement: _____

Transformation Theme: _____

Medicines: _____
_____
_____
_____

I Feel in my Body: _____
_____
_____
_____
_____
_____
_____
_____
_____

Environment/Notes: _____
_____
_____
_____
_____
_____
_____

I Feel Emotionally: _____

I Think–Beliefs/Stories/Awarenesses: _____

I Am Weaving: _____

I Intuit/Desire: _____

Date: _____ Season: _____

Day of Week: _____ Time of Day: _____ Moon Zodiac: _____

Moon Phase: _____ ○ Cycle Moon Phase: _____

Cycle Phase: _____ Cycle Season/Archetype: _____ Cycle Day: _____

Fertile: ✿ ✿ ✿ ✿ ✿ ○  PMS/Cramps: ✯ ✯ ✯ ✯ ✯  Flow: ◯ ◯ ◯ ◯ ◯

Hours of Sleep: _____ Mood: _____

Present Statement: _____

Transformation Theme: _____

Medicines: _____

I Feel in my Body: _____

Environment/Notes: _____

I Feel Emotionally: _____

I Think—Beliefs/Stories/Awarenesses: _____

I Am Weaving: _____

I Intuit/Desire: _____

Date: _____  Season: _____

Day of Week: _____  Time of Day: _____  Moon Zodiac: _____

Moon Phase: _____ ○  Cycle Moon Phase: _____

Cycle Phase: _____  Cycle Season/Archetype: _____  Cycle Day: _____

Fertile: ✿ ✿ ✿ ✿ ✿ ○   PMS/Cramps: ✦ ✦ ✦ ✦ ✦   Flow: ◊ ◊ ◊ ◊ ◊

Hours of Sleep: _____  Mood: _____

Present Statement: _____

Transformation Theme: _____

Medicines: _____

I Feel in my Body: _____

Environment/Notes: _____

*I Feel Emotionally:* _____

*I Think—Beliefs/Stories/Awarenesses:* _____

*I Am Weaving:* _____

*I Intuit/Desire:* _____

Date: _____  Season: _____

Day of Week: _____  Time of Day: _____  Moon Zodiac: _____

Moon Phase: _____ ○  Cycle Moon Phase: _____

Cycle Phase: _____  Cycle Season/Archetype: _____  Cycle Day: _____

Fertile: ✿ ✿ ✿ ✿ ✿ ○   PMS/Cramps: ☆ ☆ ☆ ☆ ☆   Flow: ◊ ◊ ◊ ◊ ◊

Hours of Sleep: _____  Mood: _____

Present Statement: _____

Transformation Theme: _____

Medicines: _____
_____
_____

I Feel in my Body: _____
_____
_____
_____
_____
_____
_____

Environment/Notes: _____
_____
_____
_____
_____
_____

I Feel Emotionally: _____

I Think–Beliefs/Stories/Awarenesses: _____

I Am Weaving: _____

I Intuit/Desire: _____

Date: _____    Season: _____

Day of Week: _____    Time of Day: _____    Moon Zodiac: _____

Moon Phase: _____    ○    Cycle Moon Phase: _____

Cycle Phase: _____    Cycle Season/Archetype: _____    Cycle Day: _____

Fertile: ✿ ✿ ✿ ✿ ✿ ○    PMS/Cramps: ☆ ☆ ☆ ☆ ☆    Flow: ◯ ◯ ◯ ◯ ◯

Hours of Sleep: _____    Mood: _____

Present Statement: _____

Transformation Theme: _____

Medicines: _____

I Feel in my Body: _____

Environment/Notes: _____

*I Feel Emotionally:* _____
_____
_____

*I Think—Beliefs/Stories/Awarenesses:* _____
_____
_____
_____
_____
_____
_____
_____
_____
_____
_____
_____
_____

*I Am Weaving:* _____
_____
_____
_____
_____
_____

*I Intuit/Desire:* _____
_____
_____
_____
_____

Date: _____  ) ● (  Season: _____

Day of Week: _____   Time of Day: _____   Moon Zodiac: _____

Moon Phase: _____  ○  Cycle Moon Phase: _____

Cycle Phase: _____   Cycle Season/Archetype: _____   Cycle Day: _____

Fertile: ✿ ✿ ✿ ✿ ✿ ○   PMS/Cramps: ✯ ✯ ✯ ✯ ✯   Flow: ◊ ◊ ◊ ◊ ◊

Hours of Sleep: _____   Mood: _____

Present Statement: _____

Transformation Theme: _____

Medicines: _____

I Feel in my Body: _____

Environment/Notes: _____

I Feel Emotionally: _____

I Think–Beliefs/Stories/Awarenesses: _____

I Am Weaving: _____

I Intuit/Desire: _____

Date: _____ Season: _____

Day of Week: _____ Time of Day: _____ Moon Zodiac: _____

Moon Phase: _____ ○ Cycle Moon Phase: _____

Cycle Phase: _____ Cycle Season/Archetype: _____ Cycle Day: _____

Fertile: ✿ ✿ ✿ ✿ ✿ ○   PMS/Cramps: ☆ ☆ ☆ ☆ ☆   Flow: ◯ ◯ ◯ ◯ ◯

Hours of Sleep: _____ Mood: _____

Present Statement: _____

Transformation Theme: _____

Medicines: _____
_____
_____
_____

I Feel in my Body: _____
_____
_____
_____
_____
_____
_____
_____

Environment/Notes: _____
_____
_____
_____
_____
_____
_____
_____

*I Feel Emotionally:*

*I Think—Beliefs/Stories/Awarenesses:*

*I Am Weaving:*

*I Intuit/Desire:*

Date: _____  Season: _____

Day of Week: _____  Time of Day: _____  Moon Zodiac: _____

Moon Phase: _____  Cycle Moon Phase: _____

Cycle Phase: _____  Cycle Season/Archetype: _____  Cycle Day: _____

Fertile: ✿ ✿ ✿ ✿ ✿ ○   PMS/Cramps: ☆ ☆ ☆ ☆ ☆   Flow: ◌ ◌ ◌ ◌ ◌

Hours of Sleep: _____  Mood: _____

Present Statement: _____

Transformation Theme: _____

Medicines: _____
_____
_____

I Feel in my Body: _____
_____
_____
_____
_____
_____
_____
_____

Environment/Notes: _____
_____
_____
_____
_____
_____

I Feel Emotionally: _____

I Think—Beliefs/Stories/Awarenesses: _____

I Am Weaving: _____

I Intuit/Desire: _____

Date: _____ Season: _____

Day of Week: _____ Time of Day: _____ Moon Zodiac: _____

Moon Phase: _____ Cycle Moon Phase: _____

Cycle Phase: _____ Cycle Season/Archetype: _____ Cycle Day: _____

Fertile: ✿ ✿ ✿ ✿ ✿ ○    PMS/Cramps: ✶ ✶ ✶ ✶ ✶    Flow: ◯ ◯ ◯ ◯ ◯

Hours of Sleep: _____ Mood: _____

Present Statement: _____

Transformation Theme: _____

Medicines: _____

I Feel in my Body: _____

Environment/Notes: _____

I Feel Emotionally: _____

I Think-Beliefs/Stories/Awarenesses: _____

I Am Weaving: _____

I Intuit/Desire: _____

Date: _____ Season: _____

Day of Week: _____ Time of Day: _____ Moon Zodiac: _____

Moon Phase: _____ Cycle Moon Phase: _____

Cycle Phase: _____ Cycle Season/Archetype: _____ Cycle Day: _____

Fertile: ✿ ✿ ✿ ✿ ✿ ○    PMS/Cramps: ☆ ☆ ☆ ☆ ☆    Flow: ◊ ◊ ◊ ◊ ◊

Hours of Sleep: _____ Mood: _____

Present Statement: _____

Transformation Theme: _____

Medicines: _____

I Feel in my Body: _____

Environment/Notes: _____

*I Feel Emotionally:*

*I Think—Beliefs/Stories/Awarenesses:*

*I Am Weaving:*

*I Intuit/Desire:*

Date: _____  ☽ ● ☾  Season: _____

Day of Week: _____  Time of Day: _____  Moon Zodiac: _____

Moon Phase: _____ ○  Cycle Moon Phase: _____

Cycle Phase: _____  Cycle Season/Archetype: _____  Cycle Day: _____

Fertile: ✿ ✿ ✿ ✿ ✿ ○   PMS/Cramps: ☆ ☆ ☆ ☆ ☆   Flow: ◊ ◊ ◊ ◊ ◊

Hours of Sleep: _____  Mood: _____

Present Statement: _____

Transformation Theme: _____

Medicines: _____

I Feel in my Body: _____

Environment/Notes: _____

**I Feel Emotionally:** _____

**I Think—Beliefs/Stories/Awarenesses:** _____

**I Am Weaving:** _____

**I Intuit/Desire:** _____

Date: _____  Season: _____

Day of Week: _____  Time of Day: _____  Moon Zodiac: _____

Moon Phase: _____  Cycle Moon Phase: _____

Cycle Phase: _____  Cycle Season/Archetype: _____  Cycle Day: _____

Fertile: ✿✿✿✿✿ ○   PMS/Cramps: ☆☆☆☆☆   Flow: ◊◊◊◊◊

Hours of Sleep: _____  Mood: _____

Present Statement: _____

Transformation Theme: _____

Medicines: _____
_____
_____

I Feel in my Body: _____
_____
_____
_____
_____
_____
_____
_____
_____

Environment/Notes: _____
_____
_____
_____
_____
_____
_____
_____

I Feel Emotionally: _____

I Think-Beliefs/Stories/Awarenesses: _____

I Am Weaving: _____

I Intuit/Desire: _____

Date: _____ Season: _____

Day of Week: _____ Time of Day: _____ Moon Zodiac: _____

Moon Phase: _____ Cycle Moon Phase: _____

Cycle Phase: _____ Cycle Season/Archetype: _____ Cycle Day: _____

Fertile: ✿ ✿ ✿ ✿ ✿ ○   PMS/Cramps: ☆ ☆ ☆ ☆ ☆   Flow: ◊ ◊ ◊ ◊ ◊

Hours of Sleep: _____ Mood: _____

Present Statement: _____

Transformation Theme: _____

Medicines: _____

I Feel in my Body: _____

Environment/Notes: _____

I Feel Emotionally: _____

I Think–Beliefs/Stories/Awarenesses: _____

I Am Weaving: _____

I Intuit/Desire: _____

Date: _____ Season: _____

Day of Week: _____ Time of Day: _____ Moon Zodiac: _____

Moon Phase: _____ ○ Cycle Moon Phase: _____

Cycle Phase: _____ Cycle Season/Archetype: _____ Cycle Day: _____

Fertile: ✿ ✿ ✿ ✿ ✿ ○    PMS/Cramps: ✧ ✧ ✧ ✧ ✧    Flow: ◊ ◊ ◊ ◊ ◊

Hours of Sleep: _____ Mood: _____

Present Statement: _____

Transformation Theme: _____

Medicines: _____

I Feel in my Body: _____

Environment/Notes: _____

*I Feel Emotionally:* _____

*I Think–Beliefs/Stories/Awarenesses:* _____

*I Am Weaving:* _____

*I Intuit/Desire:* _____

Date: _____    Season: _____

Day of Week: _____    Time of Day: _____    Moon Zodiac: _____

Moon Phase: _____ ○    Cycle Moon Phase: _____

Cycle Phase: _____    Cycle Season/Archetype: _____    Cycle Day: _____

Fertile: ✿ ✿ ✿ ✿ ✿ ○    PMS/Cramps: ✩ ✩ ✩ ✩ ✩    Flow: ◯ ◯ ◯ ◯ ◯

Hours of Sleep: _____    Mood: _____

Present Statement: _____

Transformation Theme: _____

Medicines: _____
_____
_____

I Feel in my Body: _____
_____
_____
_____
_____
_____
_____
_____

Environment/Notes: _____
_____
_____
_____
_____
_____
_____

I Feel Emotionally: _____

I Think–Beliefs/Stories/Awarenesses: _____

I Am Weaving: _____

I Intuit/Desire: _____

Date: _____  Season: _____

Day of Week: _____  Time of Day: _____  Moon Zodiac: _____

Moon Phase: _____  Cycle Moon Phase: _____

Cycle Phase: _____  Cycle Season/Archetype: _____  Cycle Day: _____

Fertile: ✿ ✿ ✿ ✿ ✿ ○  PMS/Cramps: ☆ ☆ ☆ ☆ ☆  Flow: ◯ ◯ ◯ ◯ ◯

Hours of Sleep: _____  Mood: _____

Present Statement: _____

Transformation Theme: _____

Medicines: _____

I Feel in my Body: _____

Environment/Notes: _____

*I Feel Emotionally:* _____

*I Think—Beliefs/Stories/Awarenesses:* _____

*I Am Weaving:* _____

*I Intuit/Desire:* _____

Date: _____ Season: _____

Day of Week: _____ Time of Day: _____ Moon Zodiac: _____

Moon Phase: _____ Cycle Moon Phase: _____

Cycle Phase: _____ Cycle Season/Archetype: _____ Cycle Day: _____

Fertile: ✿ ✿ ✿ ✿ ✿ ○   PMS/Cramps: ☆ ☆ ☆ ☆ ☆   Flow: ◊ ◊ ◊ ◊ ◊

Hours of Sleep: _____ Mood: _____

Present Statement: _____

Transformation Theme: _____

Medicines: _____

_____

_____

I Feel in my Body: _____

_____

_____

_____

_____

_____

_____

_____

Environment/Notes: _____

_____

_____

_____

_____

_____

I Feel Emotionally: _____

I Think-Beliefs/Stories/Awarenesses: _____

I Am Weaving: _____

I Intuit/Desire: _____

Date: _____  Season: _____

Day of Week: _____  Time of Day: _____  Moon Zodiac: _____

Moon Phase: _____  ○  Cycle Moon Phase: _____

Cycle Phase: _____  Cycle Season/Archetype: _____  Cycle Day: _____

Fertile: ✿ ✿ ✿ ✿ ✿ ○   PMS/Cramps: ☆ ☆ ☆ ☆ ☆   Flow: ◯ ◯ ◯ ◯ ◯

Hours of Sleep: _____  Mood: _____

Present Statement: _____

Transformation Theme: _____

Medicines: _____
_____
_____

I Feel in my Body: _____
_____
_____
_____
_____
_____
_____
_____

Environment/Notes: _____
_____
_____
_____
_____

**I Feel Emotionally:** _____

**I Think—Beliefs/Stories/Awarenesses:** _____

**I Am Weaving:** _____

**I Intuit/Desire:** _____

Date: _____  Season: _____

Day of Week: _____  Time of Day: _____  Moon Zodiac: _____

Moon Phase: _____  Cycle Moon Phase: _____

Cycle Phase: _____  Cycle Season/Archetype: _____  Cycle Day: _____

Fertile: ✿ ✿ ✿ ✿ ✿ ○   PMS/Cramps: ☆ ☆ ☆ ☆ ☆   Flow: ◊ ◊ ◊ ◊ ◊

Hours of Sleep: _____  Mood: _____

Present Statement: _____

Transformation Theme: _____

Medicines: _____
_____
_____

I Feel in my Body: _____
_____
_____
_____
_____
_____
_____

Environment/Notes: _____
_____
_____
_____
_____
_____

*I Feel Emotionally:* _____
_____
_____

*I Think—Beliefs/Stories/Awarenesses:* _____
_____
_____
_____
_____
_____
_____
_____
_____
_____
_____
_____
_____
_____

*I Am Weaving:* _____
_____
_____
_____
_____

*I Intuit/Desire:* _____
_____
_____
_____
_____

Date: _____ )●( Season: _____

Day of Week: _____  Time of Day: _____  Moon Zodiac: _____

Moon Phase: _____ ○ Cycle Moon Phase: _____

Cycle Phase: _____ Cycle Season/Archetype: _____ Cycle Day: _____

Fertile: ✿ ✿ ✿ ✿ ✿ ○   PMS/Cramps: ✩ ✩ ✩ ✩ ✩   Flow: ◯ ◯ ◯ ◯ ◯

Hours of Sleep: _____  Mood: _____

Present Statement: _____

Transformation Theme: _____

Medicines: _____

I Feel in my Body: _____

Environment/Notes: _____

I Feel Emotionally: _____

I Think–Beliefs/Stories/Awarenesses: _____

I Am Weaving: _____

I Intuit/Desire: _____

Date: _____ Season: _____

Day of Week: _____ Time of Day: _____ Moon Zodiac: _____

Moon Phase: _____ ○ Cycle Moon Phase: _____

Cycle Phase: _____ Cycle Season/Archetype: _____ Cycle Day: _____

Fertile: ✿✿✿✿✿ ○   PMS/Cramps: ☆☆☆☆☆   Flow: ◊◊◊◊◊

Hours of Sleep: _____ Mood: _____

Present Statement: _____

Transformation Theme: _____

Medicines: _____

I Feel in my Body: _____

Environment/Notes: _____

I Feel Emotionally: _____

I Think–Beliefs/Stories/Awarenesses: _____

I Am Weaving: _____

I Intuit/Desire: _____

Date: _____  ) ● (  Season: _____

Day of Week: _____   Time of Day: _____   Moon Zodiac: _____

Moon Phase: _____ ○   Cycle Moon Phase: _____

Cycle Phase: _____   Cycle Season/Archetype: _____   Cycle Day: _____

Fertile: ✿ ✿ ✿ ✿ ✿ ○   PMS/Cramps: ☆ ☆ ☆ ☆ ☆   Flow: ◊ ◊ ◊ ◊ ◊

Hours of Sleep: _____   Mood: _____

Present Statement: _____

Transformation Theme: _____

Medicines: _____
_____
_____
_____

I Feel in my Body: _____
_____
_____
_____
_____
_____
_____
_____
_____

Environment/Notes: _____
_____
_____
_____
_____
_____
_____
_____

**I Feel Emotionally:** _____

**I Think–Beliefs/Stories/Awarenesses:** _____

**I Am Weaving:** _____

**I Intuit/Desire:** _____

# Month 2

## Notes

**Place symbols on your calendar using this key** ⟶

- Color each circle in with the correct moon phase.
- Fill the date in the upper left corner of each square.
- Fill your cycle day in the lower right corner.

*The first day of your cycle is the first day of menstruation.*

### KEy

Flow 💧
Fertile ✿
Ovulating ○

| Sunday | Monday | Tuesday | Wednesday | Thursday | Friday | Saturday |
|--------|--------|---------|-----------|----------|--------|----------|
|        |        |         |           |          |        |          |
|        |        |         |           |          |        |          |
|        |        |         |           |          |        |          |
|        |        |         |           |          |        |          |
|        |        |         |           |          |        |          |
|        |        |         |           |          |        |          |

**Notes**

## Monthly Intuitive Desire Calendar

Use this calendar alongside your cycle and moon calendar to plan your monthly desires.

### Feminine To-Do List

- ❋ Commune with sisters
- ❋ Walk barefoot in nature
- ❋ Wear long, flowy skirts
- ❋ Sing to the trees & birds
- ❋ Hug a tree
- ❋ Smile at flowers
- ❋ Eat juicy fruit
- ❋ Put flowers in hair

# Notes

# Wheel of Transformation

# Notes

Date: _____ Season: _____

Day of Week: _____ Time of Day: _____ Moon Zodiac: _____

Moon Phase: _____ Cycle Moon Phase: _____

Cycle Phase: _____ Cycle Season/Archetype: _____ Cycle Day: _____

Fertile: ✿ ✿ ✿ ✿ ✿ ○  PMS/Cramps: ✷ ✷ ✷ ✷ ✷  Flow: ◯ ◯ ◯ ◯ ◯

Hours of Sleep: _____ Mood: _____

Present Statement: _____

Transformation Theme: _____

Medicines: _____

I Feel in my Body: _____

Environment/Notes: _____

*I Feel Emotionally:*

*I Think—Beliefs/Stories/Awarenesses:*

*I Am Weaving:*

*I Intuit/Desire:*

Date: _____ Season: _____

Day of Week: _____ Time of Day: _____ Moon Zodiac: _____

Moon Phase: _____ ○ Cycle Moon Phase: _____

Cycle Phase: _____ Cycle Season/Archetype: _____ Cycle Day: _____

Fertile: ✿ ✿ ✿ ✿ ✿ ○   PMS/Cramps: ☆ ☆ ☆ ☆ ☆   Flow: ◊ ◊ ◊ ◊ ◊

Hours of Sleep: _____ Mood: _____

Present Statement: _____

Transformation Theme: _____

Medicines: _____
_____
_____

I Feel in my Body: _____
_____
_____
_____
_____
_____
_____
_____

Environment/Notes: _____
_____
_____
_____
_____
_____

*I Feel Emotionally:* _____

*I Think—Beliefs/Stories/Awarenesses:* _____

*I Am Weaving:* _____

*I Intuit/Desire:* _____

Date: _____ Season: _____

Day of Week: _____ Time of Day: _____ Moon Zodiac: _____

Moon Phase: _____ Cycle Moon Phase: _____

Cycle Phase: _____ Cycle Season/Archetype: _____ Cycle Day: _____

Fertile: ✿ ✿ ✿ ✿ ✿ ○   PMS/Cramps: ☆ ☆ ☆ ☆ ☆   Flow: ○ ○ ○ ○ ○

Hours of Sleep: _____ Mood: _____

Present Statement: _____

Transformation Theme: _____

Medicines: _____

I Feel in my Body: _____

Environment/Notes: _____

I Feel Emotionally: _____

I Think–Beliefs/Stories/Awarenesses: _____

I Am Weaving: _____

I Intuit/Desire: _____

Date: _____ Season: _____

Day of Week: _____ Time of Day: _____ Moon Zodiac: _____

Moon Phase: _____ Cycle Moon Phase: _____

Cycle Phase: _____ Cycle Season/Archetype: _____ Cycle Day: _____

Fertile: ✿ ✿ ✿ ✿ ✿ ○   PMS/Cramps: ☆ ☆ ☆ ☆ ☆   Flow: ◯ ◯ ◯ ◯ ◯

Hours of Sleep: _____ Mood: _____

Present Statement: _____

Transformation Theme: _____

Medicines: _____
_____
_____

I Feel in my Body: _____
_____
_____
_____
_____
_____
_____
_____
_____

Environment/Notes: _____
_____
_____
_____
_____
_____
_____
_____

I Feel Emotionally: _____

I Think–Beliefs/Stories/Awarenesses: _____

I Am Weaving: _____

I Intuit/Desire: _____

Date: _____  Season: _____

Day of Week: _____  Time of Day: _____  Moon Zodiac: _____

Moon Phase: _____  Cycle Moon Phase: _____

Cycle Phase: _____  Cycle Season/Archetype: _____  Cycle Day: _____

Fertile: ✿ ✿ ✿ ✿ ✿ ○   PMS/Cramps: ☆ ☆ ☆ ☆ ☆   Flow: ○ ○ ○ ○ ○

Hours of Sleep: _____  Mood: _____

Present Statement: _____

Transformation Theme: _____

Medicines: _____
_____
_____

I Feel in my Body: _____
_____
_____
_____
_____
_____
_____
_____

Environment/Notes: _____
_____
_____
_____
_____
_____
_____
_____

**I Feel Emotionally:** _____
_____
_____

**I Think–Beliefs/Stories/Awarenesses:** _____
_____
_____
_____
_____
_____
_____
_____
_____
_____
_____
_____

**I Am Weaving:** _____
_____
_____
_____
_____

**I Intuit/Desire:** _____
_____
_____
_____
_____

Date: _____ Season: _____

Day of Week: _____ Time of Day: _____ Moon Zodiac: _____

Moon Phase: _____ ◯ Cycle Moon Phase: _____

Cycle Phase: _____ Cycle Season/Archetype: _____ Cycle Day: _____

Fertile: ✿✿✿✿✿ ◯   PMS/Cramps: ☆☆☆☆☆   Flow: ◌◌◌◌◌

Hours of Sleep: _____ Mood: _____

Present Statement: _____

Transformation Theme: _____

Medicines: _____

I Feel in my Body: _____

Environment/Notes: _____

I Feel Emotionally: _____

I Think–Beliefs/Stories/Awarenesses: _____

I Am Weaving: _____

I Intuit/Desire: _____

Date: _____   Season: _____

Day of Week: _____   Time of Day: _____   Moon Zodiac: _____

Moon Phase: _____   ○   Cycle Moon Phase: _____

Cycle Phase: _____   Cycle Season/Archetype: _____   Cycle Day: _____

Fertile: ✿ ✿ ✿ ✿ ✿ ○   PMS/Cramps: ✩ ✩ ✩ ✩ ✩   Flow: ◊ ◊ ◊ ◊ ◊

Hours of Sleep: _____   Mood: _____

Present Statement: _____

Transformation Theme: _____

Medicines: _____

I Feel in my Body: _____

Environment/Notes: _____

I Feel Emotionally: _____
_____
_____

I Think-Beliefs/Stories/Awarenesses: _____
_____
_____
_____
_____
_____
_____
_____
_____
_____
_____
_____

I Am Weaving: _____
_____
_____
_____
_____

I Intuit/Desire: _____
_____
_____
_____
_____

Date: _____ Season: _____

Day of Week: _____ Time of Day: _____ Moon Zodiac: _____

Moon Phase: _____ Cycle Moon Phase: _____

Cycle Phase: _____ Cycle Season/Archetype: _____ Cycle Day: _____

Fertile: ✿✿✿✿✿ ○   PMS/Cramps: ☆☆☆☆☆   Flow: ◊◊◊◊◊

Hours of Sleep: _____ Mood: _____

Present Statement: _____

Transformation Theme: _____

Medicines: _____

I Feel in my Body: _____

Environment/Notes: _____

**I Feel Emotionally:** _____

_____

**I Think-Beliefs/Stories/Awarenesses:** _____

_____

**I Am Weaving:** _____

_____

**I Intuit/Desire:** _____

_____

Date: _____  Season: _____

Day of Week: _____  Time of Day: _____  Moon Zodiac: _____

Moon Phase: _____  Cycle Moon Phase: _____

Cycle Phase: _____  Cycle Season/Archetype: _____  Cycle Day: _____

Fertile: ✿ ✿ ✿ ✿ ✿ ○    PMS/Cramps: ☆ ☆ ☆ ☆ ☆    Flow: ○ ○ ○ ○ ○

Hours of Sleep: _____  Mood: _____

Present Statement: _____

Transformation Theme: _____

Medicines: _____
_____
_____

I Feel in my Body: _____
_____
_____
_____
_____
_____
_____
_____

Environment/Notes: _____
_____
_____
_____
_____
_____

I Feel Emotionally: _____

I Think–Beliefs/Stories/Awarenesses: _____

I Am Weaving: _____

I Intuit/Desire: _____

Date: _____ Season: _____

Day of Week: _____ Time of Day: _____ Moon Zodiac: _____

Moon Phase: _____ ○ Cycle Moon Phase: _____

Cycle Phase: _____ Cycle Season/Archetype: _____ Cycle Day: _____

Fertile: ✿ ✿ ✿ ✿ ✿ ○   PMS/Cramps: ✯ ✯ ✯ ✯ ✯   Flow: ◌ ◌ ◌ ◌ ◌

Hours of Sleep: _____ Mood: _____

Present Statement: _____

Transformation Theme: _____

Medicines: _____

I Feel in my Body: _____

Environment/Notes: _____

I Feel Emotionally: _____

I Think–Beliefs/Stories/Awarenesses: _____

I Am Weaving: _____

I Intuit/Desire: _____

Date: _____  Season: _____

Day of Week: _____  Time of Day: _____  Moon Zodiac: _____

Moon Phase: _____ ○  Cycle Moon Phase: _____

Cycle Phase: _____  Cycle Season/Archetype: _____  Cycle Day: _____

Fertile: ✿ ✿ ✿ ✿ ✿ ○    PMS/Cramps: ☆ ☆ ☆ ☆ ☆    Flow: ◯ ◯ ◯ ◯ ◯

Hours of Sleep: _____  Mood: _____

Present Statement: _____

Transformation Theme: _____

Medicines: _____
_____
_____

I Feel in my Body: _____
_____
_____
_____
_____
_____
_____
_____

Environment/Notes: _____
_____
_____
_____
_____
_____
_____

**I Feel Emotionally:** _____

**I Think–Beliefs/Stories/Awarenesses:** _____

**I Am Weaving:** _____

**I Intuit/Desire:** _____

Date: _____ Season: _____

Day of Week: _____ Time of Day: _____ Moon Zodiac: _____

Moon Phase: _____ ○ Cycle Moon Phase: _____

Cycle Phase: _____ Cycle Season/Archetype: _____ Cycle Day: _____

Fertile: ✽ ✽ ✽ ✽ ✽ ○   PMS/Cramps: ✶ ✶ ✶ ✶ ✶   Flow: ◊ ◊ ◊ ◊ ◊

Hours of Sleep: _____ Mood: _____

Present Statement: _____

Transformation Theme: _____

Medicines: _____

_____

_____

I Feel in my Body: _____

_____

_____

_____

_____

_____

_____

_____

Environment/Notes: _____

_____

_____

_____

_____

_____

I Feel Emotionally: _____

I Think–Beliefs/Stories/Awarenesses: _____

I Am Weaving: _____

I Intuit/Desire: _____

Date: _____ Season: _____

Day of Week: _____ Time of Day: _____ Moon Zodiac: _____

Moon Phase: _____ ○ Cycle Moon Phase: _____

Cycle Phase: _____ Cycle Season/Archetype: _____ Cycle Day: _____

Fertile: ✿ ✿ ✿ ✿ ✿ ○  PMS/Cramps: ☆ ☆ ☆ ☆ ☆  Flow: ◊ ◊ ◊ ◊ ◊

Hours of Sleep: _____ Mood: _____

Present Statement: _____

Transformation Theme: _____

Medicines: _____

_____

_____

I Feel in my Body: _____

_____

_____

_____

_____

_____

_____

_____

_____

Environment/Notes: _____

_____

_____

_____

_____

_____

_____

*I Feel Emotionally:* _____

*I Think—Beliefs/Stories/Awarenesses:* _____

*I Am Weaving:* _____

*I Intuit/Desire:* _____

Date: _____  ☽●☾  Season: _____

Day of Week: _____  Time of Day: _____  Moon Zodiac: _____

Moon Phase: _____ ○  Cycle Moon Phase: _____

Cycle Phase: _____  Cycle Season/Archetype: _____  Cycle Day: _____

Fertile: ✿✿✿✿✿ ○  PMS/Cramps: ✬✬✬✬✬  Flow: ◯◯◯◯◯

Hours of Sleep: _____  Mood: _____

Present Statement: _____

Transformation Theme: _____

Medicines: _____
_____
_____
_____

I Feel in my Body: _____
_____
_____
_____
_____
_____
_____
_____
_____

Environment/Notes: _____
_____
_____
_____
_____
_____
_____
_____

**I Feel Emotionally:** _____

**I Think-Beliefs/Stories/Awarenesses:** _____

**I Am Weaving:** _____

**I Intuit/Desire:** _____

Date: _____ Season: _____

Day of Week: _____   Time of Day: _____   Moon Zodiac: _____

Moon Phase: _____   ○   Cycle Moon Phase: _____

Cycle Phase: _____   Cycle Season/Archetype: _____   Cycle Day: _____

Fertile: ✿ ✿ ✿ ✿ ✿ ○   PMS/Cramps: ☆ ☆ ☆ ☆ ☆   Flow: ◊ ◊ ◊ ◊ ◊

Hours of Sleep: _____   Mood: _____

Present Statement: _____

Transformation Theme: _____

Medicines: _____
_____
_____

I Feel in my Body: _____
_____
_____
_____
_____
_____
_____
_____

Environment/Notes: _____
_____
_____
_____
_____
_____
_____

*I Feel Emotionally:* _____

*I Think–Beliefs/Stories/Awarenesses:* _____

*I Am Weaving:* _____

*I Intuit/Desire:* _____

Date: _____  Season: _____

Day of Week: _____  Time of Day: _____  Moon Zodiac: _____

Moon Phase: _____  Cycle Moon Phase: _____

Cycle Phase: _____  Cycle Season/Archetype: _____  Cycle Day: _____

Fertile: ✿ ✿ ✿ ✿ ✿ ○   PMS/Cramps: ✦ ✦ ✦ ✦ ✦   Flow: ◊ ◊ ◊ ◊ ◊

Hours of Sleep: _____  Mood: _____

Present Statement: _____

Transformation Theme: _____

---

Medicines: _____
_____
_____

I Feel in my Body: _____
_____
_____
_____
_____
_____
_____
_____

Environment/Notes: _____
_____
_____
_____
_____
_____

I Feel Emotionally: _____

I Think–Beliefs/Stories/Awarenesses: _____

I Am Weaving: _____

I Intuit/Desire: _____

Date: _____    Season: _____

Day of Week: _____    Time of Day: _____    Moon Zodiac: _____

Moon Phase: _____    Cycle Moon Phase: _____

Cycle Phase: _____    Cycle Season/Archetype: _____    Cycle Day: _____

Fertile: ✿ ✿ ✿ ✿ ○    PMS/Cramps: ☆ ☆ ☆ ☆ ☆    Flow: ○ ○ ○ ○ ○

Hours of Sleep: _____    Mood: _____

Present Statement: _____

Transformation Theme: _____

Medicines: _____

I Feel in my Body: _____

Environment/Notes: _____

I Feel Emotionally: _____

I Think–Beliefs/Stories/Awarenesses: _____

I Am Weaving: _____

I Intuit/Desire: _____

Date: _____  Season: _____

Day of Week: _____  Time of Day: _____  Moon Zodiac: _____

Moon Phase: _____ ○  Cycle Moon Phase: _____

Cycle Phase: _____  Cycle Season/Archetype: _____  Cycle Day: _____

Fertile: ❀ ❀ ❀ ❀ ❀ ○   PMS/Cramps: ☆ ☆ ☆ ☆ ☆   Flow: ◯ ◯ ◯ ◯ ◯

Hours of Sleep: _____  Mood: _____

Present Statement: _____

Transformation Theme: _____

Medicines: _____

I Feel in my Body: _____

Environment/Notes: _____

**I Feel Emotionally:** _____

**I Think–Beliefs/Stories/Awarenesses:** _____

**I Am Weaving:** _____

**I Intuit/Desire:** _____

Date: _____ Season: _____

Day of Week: _____ Time of Day: _____ Moon Zodiac: _____

Moon Phase: _____ Cycle Moon Phase: _____

Cycle Phase: _____ Cycle Season/Archetype: _____ Cycle Day: _____

Fertile: ✿ ✿ ✿ ✿ ✿ ○    PMS/Cramps: ✯ ✯ ✯ ✯ ✯    Flow: ◯ ◯ ◯ ◯ ◯

Hours of Sleep: _____ Mood: _____

Present Statement: _____

Transformation Theme: _____

Medicines: _____

I Feel in my Body: _____

Environment/Notes: _____

I Feel Emotionally: _____

I Think–Beliefs/Stories/Awarenesses: _____

I Am Weaving: _____

I Intuit/Desire: _____

Date: _____ Season: _____

Day of Week: _____ Time of Day: _____ Moon Zodiac: _____

Moon Phase: _____ Cycle Moon Phase: _____

Cycle Phase: _____ Cycle Season/Archetype: _____ Cycle Day: _____

Fertile: ✿✿✿✿✿ ○   PMS/Cramps: ✧✧✧✧✧   Flow: ○○○○○

Hours of Sleep: _____ Mood: _____

Present Statement: _____

Transformation Theme: _____

Medicines: _____
_____
_____

I Feel in my Body: _____
_____
_____
_____
_____
_____
_____
_____
_____

Environment/Notes: _____
_____
_____
_____
_____
_____
_____

I Feel Emotionally: _____

I Think—Beliefs/Stories/Awarenesses: _____

I Am Weaving: _____

I Intuit/Desire: _____

Date: _____  Season: _____

Day of Week: _____  Time of Day: _____  Moon Zodiac: _____

Moon Phase: _____  Cycle Moon Phase: _____

Cycle Phase: _____  Cycle Season/Archetype: _____  Cycle Day: _____

Fertile: ✿ ✿ ✿ ✿ ✿ ○   PMS/Cramps: ☆ ☆ ☆ ☆ ☆   Flow: ◯ ◯ ◯ ◯ ◯

Hours of Sleep: _____  Mood: _____

Present Statement: _____

Transformation Theme: _____

Medicines: _____
_____
_____

I Feel in my Body: _____
_____
_____
_____
_____
_____
_____
_____
_____

Environment/Notes: _____
_____
_____
_____
_____
_____
_____

I Feel Emotionally: _____

I Think-Beliefs/Stories/Awarenesses: _____

I Am Weaving: _____

I Intuit/Desire: _____

Date: _____ ))●(( Season: _____

Day of Week: _____ Time of Day: _____ Moon Zodiac: _____

Moon Phase: _____ ○ Cycle Moon Phase: _____

Cycle Phase: _____ Cycle Season/Archetype: _____ Cycle Day: _____

Fertile: ✿ ✿ ✿ ✿ ✿ ○  PMS/Cramps: ☆ ☆ ☆ ☆ ☆  Flow: ○ ○ ○ ○ ○

Hours of Sleep: _____ Mood: _____

Present Statement: _____

Transformation Theme: _____

Medicines: _____

I Feel in my Body: _____

Environment/Notes: _____

I Feel Emotionally: _____

I Think–Beliefs/Stories/Awarenesses: _____

I Am Weaving: _____

I Intuit/Desire: _____

Date: _____  Season: _____

Day of Week: _____  Time of Day: _____  Moon Zodiac: _____

Moon Phase: _____ ○  Cycle Moon Phase: _____

Cycle Phase: _____  Cycle Season/Archetype: _____  Cycle Day: _____

Fertile: ✿ ✿ ✿ ✿ ✿ ○   PMS/Cramps: ✩ ✩ ✩ ✩ ✩   Flow: ◊ ◊ ◊ ◊ ◊

Hours of Sleep: _____  Mood: _____

Present Statement: _____

Transformation Theme: _____

---

Medicines: _____
_____
_____
_____

I Feel in my Body: _____
_____
_____
_____
_____
_____
_____
_____
_____

Environment/Notes: _____
_____
_____
_____
_____
_____
_____
_____

I Feel Emotionally: _____

I Think—Beliefs/Stories/Awarenesses: _____

I Am Weaving: _____

I Intuit/Desire: _____

Date: _____  Season: _____

Day of Week: _____  Time of Day: _____  Moon Zodiac: _____

Moon Phase: _____  ◯  Cycle Moon Phase: _____

Cycle Phase: _____  Cycle Season/Archetype: _____  Cycle Day: _____

Fertile: ✿ ✿ ✿ ✿ ✿ ◯     PMS/Cramps: ✩ ✩ ✩ ✩ ✩     Flow: ◊ ◊ ◊ ◊ ◊

Hours of Sleep: _____  Mood: _____

Present Statement: _____

Transformation Theme: _____

Medicines: _____

I Feel in my Body: _____

Environment/Notes: _____

I Feel Emotionally: _____

I Think–Beliefs/Stories/Awarenesses: _____

I Am Weaving: _____

I Intuit/Desire: _____

Date: _____  Season: _____

Day of Week: _____  Time of Day: _____  Moon Zodiac: _____

Moon Phase: _____  Cycle Moon Phase: _____

Cycle Phase: _____  Cycle Season/Archetype: _____  Cycle Day: _____

Fertile: ✿ ✿ ✿ ✿ ✿ ○   PMS/Cramps: ✯ ✯ ✯ ✯ ✯   Flow: ◊ ◊ ◊ ◊ ◊

Hours of Sleep: _____  Mood: _____

Present Statement: _____

Transformation Theme: _____

_____

Medicines: _____

_____

_____

I Feel in my Body: _____

_____
_____
_____
_____
_____
_____
_____
_____

Environment/Notes: _____

_____
_____
_____
_____
_____
_____
_____

I Feel Emotionally: _____

I Think-Beliefs/Stories/Awarenesses: _____

I Am Weaving: _____

I Intuit/Desire: _____

Date: _____ Season: _____

Day of Week: _____ Time of Day: _____ Moon Zodiac: _____

Moon Phase: _____ ○ Cycle Moon Phase: _____

Cycle Phase: _____ Cycle Season/Archetype: _____ Cycle Day: _____

Fertile: ✿ ✿ ✿ ✿ ✿ ○   PMS/Cramps: ☆ ☆ ☆ ☆ ☆   Flow: ○ ○ ○ ○ ○

Hours of Sleep: _____ Mood: _____

Present Statement: _____

Transformation Theme: _____

Medicines: _____

I Feel in my Body: _____

Environment/Notes: _____

I Feel Emotionally: _____
_____
_____

I Think–Beliefs/Stories/Awarenesses: _____
_____
_____
_____
_____
_____
_____
_____
_____
_____
_____

I Am Weaving: _____
_____
_____
_____
_____

I Intuit/Desire: _____
_____
_____
_____

Date: _____ Season: _____

Day of Week: _____ Time of Day: _____ Moon Zodiac: _____

Moon Phase: _____ ○ Cycle Moon Phase: _____

Cycle Phase: _____ Cycle Season/Archetype: _____ Cycle Day: _____

Fertile: ✿ ✿ ✿ ✿ ✿ ○   PMS/Cramps: ✦ ✦ ✦ ✦ ✦   Flow: ◯ ◯ ◯ ◯ ◯

Hours of Sleep: _____ Mood: _____

Present Statement: _____

Transformation Theme: _____

Medicines: _____

I Feel in my Body: _____

Environment/Notes: _____

I Feel Emotionally: _____

I Think-Beliefs/Stories/Awarenesses: _____

I Am Weaving: _____

I Intuit/Desire: _____

Date: _____  Season: _____

Day of Week: _____  Time of Day: _____  Moon Zodiac: _____

Moon Phase: _____  Cycle Moon Phase: _____

Cycle Phase: _____  Cycle Season/Archetype: _____  Cycle Day: _____

Fertile: ✿ ✿ ✿ ✿ ✿ ○   PMS/Cramps: ☆ ☆ ☆ ☆ ☆   Flow: ○ ○ ○ ○ ○

Hours of Sleep: _____  Mood: _____

Present Statement: _____

Transformation Theme: _____

Medicines: _____

I Feel in my Body: _____

Environment/Notes: _____

I Feel Emotionally:

I Think-Beliefs/Stories/Awarenesses:

I Am Weaving:

I Intuit/Desire:

Date: _____ Season: _____

Day of Week: _____  Time of Day: _____  Moon Zodiac: _____

Moon Phase: _____ ◯  Cycle Moon Phase: _____

Cycle Phase: _____  Cycle Season/Archetype: _____  Cycle Day: _____

Fertile: ✿ ✿ ✿ ✿ ✿ ◯    PMS/Cramps: ☆ ☆ ☆ ☆ ☆    Flow: ◯ ◯ ◯ ◯ ◯

Hours of Sleep: _____  Mood: _____

Present Statement: _____

Transformation Theme: _____

Medicines: _____
_____
_____

I Feel in my Body: _____
_____
_____
_____
_____
_____
_____
_____

Environment/Notes: _____
_____
_____
_____
_____
_____
_____

I Feel Emotionally: _____

I Think—Beliefs/Stories/Awarenesses: _____

I Am Weaving: _____

I Intuit/Desire: _____

Date: _____ Season: _____

Day of Week: _____ Time of Day: _____ Moon Zodiac: _____

Moon Phase: _____ Cycle Moon Phase: _____

Cycle Phase: _____ Cycle Season/Archetype: _____ Cycle Day: _____

Fertile: ✿✿✿✿✿ ○   PMS/Cramps: ☆☆☆☆☆   Flow: ♦♦♦♦♦

Hours of Sleep: _____ Mood: _____

Present Statement: _____

Transformation Theme: _____

Medicines: _____

I Feel in my Body: _____

Environment/Notes: _____

I Feel Emotionally:

I Think-Beliefs/Stories/Awarenesses:

I Am Weaving:

I Intuit/Desire:

Date: _____  Season: _____

Day of Week: _____  Time of Day: _____  Moon Zodiac: _____

Moon Phase: _____  Cycle Moon Phase: _____

Cycle Phase: _____  Cycle Season/Archetype: _____  Cycle Day: _____

Fertile: ✿ ✿ ✿ ✿ ✿ ○   PMS/Cramps: ☆ ☆ ☆ ☆ ☆   Flow: ◯ ◯ ◯ ◯ ◯

Hours of Sleep: _____  Mood: _____

Present Statement: _____

Transformation Theme: _____

Medicines: _____

I Feel in my Body: _____

Environment/Notes: _____

I Feel Emotionally: _____
_____
_____

I Think–Beliefs/Stories/Awarenesses: _____
_____
_____
_____
_____
_____
_____
_____
_____
_____
_____
_____
_____
_____

I Am Weaving: _____
_____
_____
_____
_____
_____

I Intuit/Desire: _____
_____
_____
_____
_____
_____

# Month 3

**Place symbols on your calendar using this key** →

- Color each circle in with the correct moon phase.
- Fill the date in the upper left corner of each square.
- Fill your cycle day in the lower right corner.

*The first day of your cycle is the first day of menstruation.*

### Key
Flow 💧
Fertile ❀
Ovulating ○

| Sunday | Monday | Tuesday | Wednesday | Thursday | Friday | Saturday |
|---|---|---|---|---|---|---|
|  |  |  |  |  |  |  |
|  |  |  |  |  |  |  |
|  |  |  |  |  |  |  |
|  |  |  |  |  |  |  |
|  |  |  |  |  |  |  |
|  |  |  |  |  |  |  |

**Notes**

*Monthly Intuitive Desire Calendar*

Use this calendar alongside your cycle and moon calendar to plan your monthly desires.

### Feminine To-Do List

- ❋ Commune with sisters
- ❋ Walk barefoot in nature
- ❋ Wear long, flowy skirts
- ❋ Sing to the trees & birds
- ❋ Hug a tree
- ❋ Smile at flowers
- ❋ Eat juicy fruit
- ❋ Put flowers in hair

# Notes

# Wheel of Transformation

# Notes

Date: _____ ☽ ● ☾ Season: _____

Day of Week: _____  Time of Day: _____  Moon Zodiac: _____

Moon Phase: _____ ○  Cycle Moon Phase: _____

Cycle Phase: _____  Cycle Season/Archetype: _____  Cycle Day: _____

Fertile: ✿ ✿ ✿ ✿ ✿ ○   PMS/Cramps: ☆ ☆ ☆ ☆ ☆   Flow: ◯ ◯ ◯ ◯ ◯

Hours of Sleep: _____  Mood: _____

Present Statement: _____

Transformation Theme: _____
_____

Medicines: _____
_____
_____

I Feel in my Body: _____
_____
_____
_____
_____
_____
_____
_____
_____

Environment/Notes: _____
_____
_____
_____
_____
_____
_____

*I Feel Emotionally:*

*I Think—Beliefs/Stories/Awarenesses:*

*I Am Weaving:*

*I Intuit/Desire:*

Date: _____ Season: _____

Day of Week: _____ Time of Day: _____ Moon Zodiac: _____

Moon Phase: _____ Cycle Moon Phase: _____

Cycle Phase: _____ Cycle Season/Archetype: _____ Cycle Day: _____

Fertile: ✿ ✿ ✿ ✿ ✿ ○   PMS/Cramps: ☆ ☆ ☆ ☆ ☆   Flow: ◊ ◊ ◊ ◊ ◊

Hours of Sleep: _____ Mood: _____

Present Statement: _____

Transformation Theme: _____

---

Medicines: _____
_____
_____

I Feel in my Body: _____
_____
_____
_____
_____
_____
_____
_____

Environment/Notes: _____
_____
_____
_____
_____
_____
_____

I Feel Emotionally: _____

I Think–Beliefs/Stories/Awarenesses: _____

I Am Weaving: _____

I Intuit/Desire: _____

Date: _____ Season: _____

Day of Week: _____ Time of Day: _____ Moon Zodiac: _____

Moon Phase: _____ ○ Cycle Moon Phase: _____

Cycle Phase: _____ Cycle Season/Archetype: _____ Cycle Day: _____

Fertile: ✿✿✿✿✿ ○     PMS/Cramps: ✦✦✦✦✦     Flow: ◊◊◊◊◊

Hours of Sleep: _____ Mood: _____

Present Statement: _____

Transformation Theme: _____

Medicines: _____

I Feel in my Body: _____

Environment/Notes: _____

*I Feel Emotionally:* _____

*I Think—Beliefs/Stories/Awarenesses:* _____

*I Am Weaving:* _____

*I Intuit/Desire:* _____

Date: _____ ) ● ( Season: _____

Day of Week: _____  Time of Day: _____  Moon Zodiac: _____

Moon Phase: _____ ○  Cycle Moon Phase: _____

Cycle Phase: _____  Cycle Season/Archetype: _____  Cycle Day: _____

Fertile: ✿✿✿✿✿ ○  PMS/Cramps: ☆☆☆☆☆  Flow: ◯◯◯◯◯

Hours of Sleep: _____  Mood: _____

Present Statement: _____

Transformation Theme: _____

Medicines: _____
_____
_____

I Feel in my Body: _____
_____
_____
_____
_____
_____
_____
_____

Environment/Notes: _____
_____
_____
_____
_____
_____
_____

I Feel Emotionally: _____
_____
_____

I Think–Beliefs/Stories/Awarenesses: _____
_____
_____
_____
_____
_____
_____
_____
_____
_____
_____

I Am Weaving: _____
_____
_____
_____
_____

I Intuit/Desire: _____
_____
_____
_____
_____

Date: _____ Season: _____

Day of Week: _____ Time of Day: _____ Moon Zodiac: _____

Moon Phase: _____ ◯ Cycle Moon Phase: _____

Cycle Phase: _____ Cycle Season/Archetype: _____ Cycle Day: _____

Fertile: ✿ ✿ ✿ ✿ ✿ ◯    PMS/Cramps: ☆ ☆ ☆ ☆ ☆    Flow: ◊ ◊ ◊ ◊ ◊

Hours of Sleep: _____ Mood: _____

Present Statement: _____

Transformation Theme: _____

Medicines: _____
_____
_____

I Feel in my Body: _____
_____
_____
_____
_____
_____
_____
_____

Environment/Notes: _____
_____
_____
_____
_____
_____
_____

I Feel Emotionally: _____

I Think—Beliefs/Stories/Awarenesses: _____

I Am Weaving: _____

I Intuit/Desire: _____

Date: _____  Season: _____

Day of Week: _____  Time of Day: _____  Moon Zodiac: _____

Moon Phase: _____  Cycle Moon Phase: _____

Cycle Phase: _____  Cycle Season/Archetype: _____  Cycle Day: _____

Fertile: ✿✿✿✿✿ ○  PMS/Cramps: ☆☆☆☆☆  Flow: ○○○○○

Hours of Sleep: _____  Mood: _____

Present Statement: _____

Transformation Theme: _____

Medicines: _____

I Feel in my Body: _____

Environment/Notes: _____

I Feel Emotionally: _____

I Think—Beliefs/Stories/Awarenesses: _____

I Am Weaving: _____

I Intuit/Desire: _____

Date: _____  Season: _____

Day of Week: _____  Time of Day: _____  Moon Zodiac: _____

Moon Phase: _____  Cycle Moon Phase: _____

Cycle Phase: _____  Cycle Season/Archetype: _____  Cycle Day: _____

Fertile: ✿ ✿ ✿ ✿ ✿ ○   PMS/Cramps: ☆ ☆ ☆ ☆ ☆   Flow: ◊ ◊ ◊ ◊ ◊

Hours of Sleep: _____  Mood: _____

Present Statement: _____

Transformation Theme: _____

Medicines: _____
_____
_____

I Feel in my Body: _____
_____
_____
_____
_____
_____
_____
_____

Environment/Notes: _____
_____
_____
_____
_____
_____
_____

I Feel Emotionally: _____

I Think-Beliefs/Stories/Awarenesses: _____

I Am Weaving: _____

I Intuit/Desire: _____

Date: _____  ☽●☾  Season: _____

Day of Week: _____  Time of Day: _____  Moon Zodiac: _____

Moon Phase: _____ ○  Cycle Moon Phase: _____

Cycle Phase: _____  Cycle Season/Archetype: _____  Cycle Day: _____

Fertile: ✿✿✿✿✿○  PMS/Cramps: ☆☆☆☆☆  Flow: ○○○○○

Hours of Sleep: _____  Mood: _____

Present Statement: _____

Transformation Theme: _____

Medicines: _____
_____
_____
_____

I Feel in my Body: _____
_____
_____
_____
_____
_____
_____
_____
_____
_____

Environment/Notes: _____
_____
_____
_____
_____
_____
_____
_____

**I Feel Emotionally:**

**I Think—Beliefs/Stories/Awarenesses:**

**I Am Weaving:**

**I Intuit/Desire:**

Date: _____ Season: _____

Day of Week: _____ Time of Day: _____ Moon Zodiac: _____

Moon Phase: _____ Cycle Moon Phase: _____

Cycle Phase: _____ Cycle Season/Archetype: _____ Cycle Day: _____

Fertile: ✿ ✿ ✿ ✿ ✿ ○    PMS/Cramps: ☆ ☆ ☆ ☆ ☆    Flow: ◊ ◊ ◊ ◊ ◊

Hours of Sleep: _____ Mood: _____

Present Statement: _____

Transformation Theme: _____

Medicines: _____
_____
_____

I Feel in my Body: _____
_____
_____
_____
_____
_____
_____
_____
_____

Environment/Notes: _____
_____
_____
_____
_____
_____
_____
_____

I Feel Emotionally: _____

I Think–Beliefs/Stories/Awarenesses: _____

I Am Weaving: _____

I Intuit/Desire: _____

Date: _____ Season: _____

Day of Week: _____ Time of Day: _____ Moon Zodiac: _____

Moon Phase: _____ ◯ Cycle Moon Phase: _____

Cycle Phase: _____ Cycle Season/Archetype: _____ Cycle Day: _____

Fertile: ✿ ✿ ✿ ✿ ✿ ◯   PMS/Cramps: ✡ ✡ ✡ ✡ ✡   Flow: ◊ ◊ ◊ ◊ ◊

Hours of Sleep: _____ Mood: _____

Present Statement: _____

Transformation Theme: _____

Medicines: _____
_____
_____

I Feel in my Body: _____
_____
_____
_____
_____
_____
_____
_____
_____

Environment/Notes: _____
_____
_____
_____
_____
_____
_____

I Feel Emotionally: _____
_____
_____

I Think–Beliefs/Stories/Awarenesses: _____
_____
_____
_____
_____
_____
_____
_____
_____
_____
_____
_____

I Am Weaving: _____
_____
_____
_____
_____

I Intuit/Desire: _____
_____
_____
_____
_____

Date: _____ Season: _____

Day of Week: _____ Time of Day: _____ Moon Zodiac: _____

Moon Phase: _____ ○ Cycle Moon Phase: _____

Cycle Phase: _____ Cycle Season/Archetype: _____ Cycle Day: _____

Fertile: ✿ ✿ ✿ ✿ ✿ ○   PMS/Cramps: ✦ ✦ ✦ ✦ ✦   Flow: ◯ ◯ ◯ ◯ ◯

Hours of Sleep: _____ Mood: _____

Present Statement: _____

Transformation Theme: _____

Medicines: _____
_____
_____

I Feel in my Body: _____
_____
_____
_____
_____
_____
_____
_____

Environment/Notes: _____
_____
_____
_____
_____
_____
_____

I Feel Emotionally: _____

I Think-Beliefs/Stories/Awarenesses: _____

I Am Weaving: _____

I Intuit/Desire: _____

Date: _____ Season: _____

Day of Week: _____  Time of Day: _____  Moon Zodiac: _____

Moon Phase: _____ ○  Cycle Moon Phase: _____

Cycle Phase: _____  Cycle Season/Archetype: _____  Cycle Day: _____

Fertile: ✿ ✿ ✿ ✿ ✿ ○   PMS/Cramps: ☆ ☆ ☆ ☆ ☆   Flow: ◯ ◯ ◯ ◯ ◯

Hours of Sleep: _____  Mood: _____

Present Statement: _____

Transformation Theme: _____

Medicines: _____
_____
_____

I Feel in my Body: _____
_____
_____
_____
_____
_____
_____
_____
_____

Environment/Notes: _____
_____
_____
_____
_____
_____
_____
_____

I Feel Emotionally: _____

I Think–Beliefs/Stories/Awarenesses: _____

I Am Weaving: _____

I Intuit/Desire: _____

Date: _____ ☽ ● ☾ Season: _____

Day of Week: _____  Time of Day: _____  Moon Zodiac: _____

Moon Phase: _____ ○  Cycle Moon Phase: _____

Cycle Phase: _____  Cycle Season/Archetype: _____  Cycle Day: _____

Fertile: ✿ ✿ ✿ ✿ ✿ ○   PMS/Cramps: ☆ ☆ ☆ ☆ ☆   Flow: ◊ ◊ ◊ ◊ ◊

Hours of Sleep: _____  Mood: _____

Present Statement: _____

Transformation Theme: _____

Medicines: _____

I Feel in my Body: _____

Environment/Notes: _____

I Feel Emotionally: _____

I Think-Beliefs/Stories/Awarenesses: _____

I Am Weaving: _____

I Intuit/Desire: _____

Date: _____ Season: _____

Day of Week: _____ Time of Day: _____ Moon Zodiac: _____

Moon Phase: _____ Cycle Moon Phase: _____

Cycle Phase: _____ Cycle Season/Archetype: _____ Cycle Day: _____

Fertile: ✿ ✿ ✿ ✿ ✿ ○   PMS/Cramps: ✦ ✦ ✦ ✦ ✦   Flow: ◊ ◊ ◊ ◊ ◊

Hours of Sleep: _____ Mood: _____

Present Statement: _____

Transformation Theme: _____

Medicines: _____

I Feel in my Body: _____

Environment/Notes: _____

*I Feel Emotionally:*

*I Think–Beliefs/Stories/Awarenesses:*

*I Am Weaving:*

*I Intuit/Desire:*

Date: _____ Season: _____

Day of Week: _____ Time of Day: _____ Moon Zodiac: _____

Moon Phase: _____ Cycle Moon Phase: _____

Cycle Phase: _____ Cycle Season/Archetype: _____ Cycle Day: _____

Fertile: ✿✿✿✿✿ ○   PMS/Cramps: ✫✫✫✫✫   Flow: ◊◊◊◊◊

Hours of Sleep: _____ Mood: _____

Present Statement: _____

Transformation Theme: _____

Medicines: _____

I Feel in my Body: _____

Environment/Notes: _____

I Feel Emotionally: _____

I Think-Beliefs/Stories/Awarenesses: _____

I Am Weaving: _____

I Intuit/Desire: _____

Date: _____  Season: _____

Day of Week: _____  Time of Day: _____  Moon Zodiac: _____

Moon Phase: _____  Cycle Moon Phase: _____

Cycle Phase: _____  Cycle Season/Archetype: _____  Cycle Day: _____

Fertile: ✿ ✿ ✿ ✿ ✿ ○   PMS/Cramps: ☆ ☆ ☆ ☆ ☆   Flow: ○ ○ ○ ○ ○

Hours of Sleep: _____  Mood: _____

Present Statement: _____

Transformation Theme: _____

Medicines: _____
_____
_____

I Feel in my Body: _____
_____
_____
_____
_____
_____
_____
_____

Environment/Notes: _____
_____
_____
_____
_____
_____

I Feel Emotionally: _____
_____
_____

I Think–Beliefs/Stories/Awarenesses: _____
_____
_____
_____
_____
_____
_____
_____
_____
_____
_____
_____
_____
_____

I Am Weaving: _____
_____
_____
_____
_____

I Intuit/Desire: _____
_____
_____
_____
_____

Date: _____  Season: _____

Day of Week: _____  Time of Day: _____  Moon Zodiac: _____

Moon Phase: _____  Cycle Moon Phase: _____

Cycle Phase: _____  Cycle Season/Archetype: _____  Cycle Day: _____

Fertile: ✿ ✿ ✿ ✿ ✿ ○   PMS/Cramps: ☆ ☆ ☆ ☆ ☆   Flow: ◊ ◊ ◊ ◊ ◊

Hours of Sleep: _____  Mood: _____

Present Statement: _____

Transformation Theme: _____

Medicines: _____

I Feel in my Body: _____

Environment/Notes: _____

I Feel Emotionally:

I Think–Beliefs/Stories/Awarenesses:

I Am Weaving:

I Intuit/Desire:

Date: _____ ))(( Season: _____

Day of Week: _____  Time of Day: _____  Moon Zodiac: _____

Moon Phase: _____ ◯ Cycle Moon Phase: _____

Cycle Phase: _____  Cycle Season/Archetype: _____  Cycle Day: _____

Fertile: ✿✿✿✿✿ ◯   PMS/Cramps: ✶✶✶✶✶   Flow: ◊◊◊◊◊

Hours of Sleep: _____   Mood: _____

Present Statement: _____

Transformation Theme: _____

---

Medicines: _____
_____
_____

I Feel in my Body: _____
_____
_____
_____
_____
_____
_____
_____
_____

Environment/Notes: _____
_____
_____
_____
_____
_____
_____

I Feel Emotionally:

I Think-Beliefs/Stories/Awarenesses:

I Am Weaving:

I Intuit/Desire:

Date: _____  Season: _____

Day of Week: _____  Time of Day: _____  Moon Zodiac: _____

Moon Phase: _____  Cycle Moon Phase: _____

Cycle Phase: _____  Cycle Season/Archetype: _____  Cycle Day: _____

Fertile: ✿ ✿ ✿ ✿ ✿ ○    PMS/Cramps: ☆ ☆ ☆ ☆ ☆    Flow: ◯ ◯ ◯ ◯

Hours of Sleep: _____  Mood: _____

Present Statement: _____

Transformation Theme: _____

Medicines: _____

I Feel in my Body: _____

Environment/Notes: _____

I Feel Emotionally: _____

I Think—Beliefs/Stories/Awarenesses: _____

I Am Weaving: _____

I Intuit/Desire: _____

Date: _____ Season: _____

Day of Week: _____ Time of Day: _____ Moon Zodiac: _____

Moon Phase: _____ Cycle Moon Phase: _____

Cycle Phase: _____ Cycle Season/Archetype: _____ Cycle Day: _____

Fertile: ✿ ✿ ✿ ✿ ✿ ○   PMS/Cramps: ☆ ☆ ☆ ☆ ☆   Flow: ○ ○ ○ ○ ○

Hours of Sleep: _____ Mood: _____

Present Statement: _____

Transformation Theme: _____

Medicines: _____

I Feel in my Body: _____

Environment/Notes: _____

I Feel Emotionally: _____

I Think–Beliefs/Stories/Awarenesses: _____

I Am Weaving: _____

I Intuit/Desire: _____

Date: _____ Season: _____

Day of Week: _____ Time of Day: _____ Moon Zodiac: _____

Moon Phase: _____ Cycle Moon Phase: _____

Cycle Phase: _____ Cycle Season/Archetype: _____ Cycle Day: _____

Fertile: ✿✿✿✿✿ ○  PMS/Cramps: ☆☆☆☆☆  Flow: ○○○○○

Hours of Sleep: _____ Mood: _____

Present Statement: _____

Transformation Theme: _____

Medicines: _____

I Feel in my Body: _____

Environment/Notes: _____

I Feel Emotionally: _____
_____
_____

I Think–Beliefs/Stories/Awarenesses: _____
_____
_____
_____
_____
_____
_____
_____
_____
_____
_____
_____

I Am Weaving: _____
_____
_____
_____
_____

I Intuit/Desire: _____
_____
_____
_____
_____

Date: _____ Season: _____

Day of Week: _____ Time of Day: _____ Moon Zodiac: _____

Moon Phase: _____ Cycle Moon Phase: _____

Cycle Phase: _____ Cycle Season/Archetype: _____ Cycle Day: _____

Fertile: ✿✿✿✿✿ ○          PMS/Cramps: ✦✦✦✦✦          Flow: ◊◊◊◊◊

Hours of Sleep: _____ Mood: _____

Present Statement: _____

Transformation Theme: _____

Medicines: _____

I Feel in my Body: _____

Environment/Notes: _____

I Feel Emotionally: _____
_____
_____

I Think–Beliefs/Stories/Awarenesses: _____
_____
_____
_____
_____
_____
_____
_____
_____
_____
_____
_____

I Am Weaving: _____
_____
_____
_____
_____
_____

I Intuit/Desire: _____
_____
_____
_____
_____

Date: _____ Season: _____

Day of Week: _____ Time of Day: _____ Moon Zodiac: _____

Moon Phase: _____ ○ Cycle Moon Phase: _____

Cycle Phase: _____ Cycle Season/Archetype: _____ Cycle Day: _____

Fertile: ✿ ✿ ✿ ✿ ✿ ○     PMS/Cramps: ☆ ☆ ☆ ☆ ☆     Flow: ◊ ◊ ◊ ◊ ◊

Hours of Sleep: _____ Mood: _____

Present Statement: _____

Transformation Theme: _____

Medicines: _____

I Feel in my Body: _____

Environment/Notes: _____

I Feel Emotionally:

I Think-Beliefs/Stories/Awarenesses:

I Am Weaving:

I Intuit/Desire:

Date: _____ ))◐(( Season: _____

Day of Week: _____ Time of Day: _____ Moon Zodiac: _____

Moon Phase: _____ ○ Cycle Moon Phase: _____

Cycle Phase: _____ Cycle Season/Archetype: _____ Cycle Day: _____

Fertile: ✿ ✿ ✿ ✿ ✿ ○   PMS/Cramps: ☆ ☆ ☆ ☆ ☆   Flow: ○ ○ ○ ○ ○

Hours of Sleep: _____ Mood: _____

Present Statement: _____

Transformation Theme: _____

Medicines: _____
_____
_____
_____

I Feel in my Body: _____
_____
_____
_____
_____
_____
_____
_____
_____

Environment/Notes: _____
_____
_____
_____
_____
_____
_____
_____

I Feel Emotionally: _____

I Think-Beliefs/Stories/Awarenesses: _____

I Am Weaving: _____

I Intuit/Desire: _____

Date: _____ Season: _____

Day of Week: _____ Time of Day: _____ Moon Zodiac: _____

Moon Phase: _____ Cycle Moon Phase: _____

Cycle Phase: _____ Cycle Season/Archetype: _____ Cycle Day: _____

Fertile: ✿✿✿✿✿ ○   PMS/Cramps: ✬✬✬✬✬   Flow: ◊◊◊◊◊

Hours of Sleep: _____ Mood: _____

Present Statement: _____

Transformation Theme: _____

Medicines: _____

I Feel in my Body: _____

Environment/Notes: _____

I Feel Emotionally: _____
_____

I Think–Beliefs/Stories/Awarenesses: _____
_____
_____
_____
_____
_____
_____
_____
_____
_____

I Am Weaving: _____
_____
_____
_____
_____

I Intuit/Desire: _____
_____
_____
_____

Date: _____ Season: _____

Day of Week: _____ Time of Day: _____ Moon Zodiac: _____

Moon Phase: _____ Cycle Moon Phase: _____

Cycle Phase: _____ Cycle Season/Archetype: _____ Cycle Day: _____

Fertile: ✿ ✿ ✿ ✿ ✿ ○   PMS/Cramps: ☆ ☆ ☆ ☆ ☆   Flow: ◯ ◯ ◯ ◯ ◯

Hours of Sleep: _____ Mood: _____

Present Statement: _____

Transformation Theme: _____

Medicines: _____

I Feel in my Body: _____

Environment/Notes: _____

I Feel Emotionally: _____

I Think-Beliefs/Stories/Awarenesses: _____

I Am Weaving: _____

I Intuit/Desire: _____

Date: _____  Season: _____

Day of Week: _____  Time of Day: _____  Moon Zodiac: _____

Moon Phase: _____  Cycle Moon Phase: _____

Cycle Phase: _____  Cycle Season/Archetype: _____  Cycle Day: _____

Fertile: ✿ ✿ ✿ ✿ ✿ ○   PMS/Cramps: ✭ ✭ ✭ ✭ ✭   Flow: ◊ ◊ ◊ ◊ ◊

Hours of Sleep: _____  Mood: _____

Present Statement: _____

Transformation Theme: _____

Medicines: _____

I Feel in my Body: _____

Environment/Notes: _____

I Feel Emotionally:

I Think-Beliefs/Stories/Awarenesses:

I Am Weaving:

I Intuit/Desire:

Date: _____ Season: _____

Day of Week: _____ Time of Day: _____ Moon Zodiac: _____

Moon Phase: _____ Cycle Moon Phase: _____

Cycle Phase: _____ Cycle Season/Archetype: _____ Cycle Day: _____

Fertile: ✿ ✿ ✿ ✿ ✿ ○   PMS/Cramps: ✰ ✰ ✰ ✰ ✰   Flow: ◊ ◊ ◊ ◊

Hours of Sleep: _____ Mood: _____

Present Statement: _____

Transformation Theme: _____

---

Medicines: _____

I Feel in my Body: _____

Environment/Notes: _____

I Feel Emotionally: _____

I Think–Beliefs/Stories/Awarenesses: _____

I Am Weaving: _____

I Intuit/Desire: _____

Date: _____  ☽●☾  Season: _____

Day of Week: _____   Time of Day: _____   Moon Zodiac: _____

Moon Phase: _____ ○   Cycle Moon Phase: _____

Cycle Phase: _____   Cycle Season/Archetype: _____   Cycle Day: _____

Fertile: ✿ ✿ ✿ ✿ ✿ ○   PMS/Cramps: ✦ ✦ ✦ ✦ ✦   Flow: ◯ ◯ ◯ ◯ ◯

Hours of Sleep: _____   Mood: _____

Present Statement: _____
Transformation Theme: _____

Medicines: _____
_____
_____
_____

I Feel in my Body: _____
_____
_____
_____
_____
_____
_____
_____
_____

Environment/Notes: _____
_____
_____
_____
_____
_____
_____
_____

*I Feel Emotionally:*

*I Think–Beliefs/Stories/Awarenesses:*

*I Am Weaving:*

*I Intuit/Desire:*

Date: _____ Season: _____

Day of Week: _____ Time of Day: _____ Moon Zodiac: _____

Moon Phase: _____ Cycle Moon Phase: _____

Cycle Phase: _____ Cycle Season/Archetype: _____ Cycle Day: _____

Fertile: ✿ ✿ ✿ ✿ ✿ ○   PMS/Cramps: ☆ ☆ ☆ ☆ ☆   Flow: ◊ ◊ ◊ ◊ ◊

Hours of Sleep: _____ Mood: _____

Present Statement: _____

Transformation Theme: _____

Medicines: _____
_____
_____

I Feel in my Body: _____
_____
_____
_____
_____
_____
_____
_____
_____

Environment/Notes: _____
_____
_____
_____
_____
_____
_____

I Feel Emotionally: _____

I Think–Beliefs/Stories/Awarenesses: _____

I Am Weaving: _____

I Intuit/Desire: _____

Date: _____ ) ● ( Season: _____

Day of Week: _____ Time of Day: _____ Moon Zodiac: _____

Moon Phase: _____ ○ Cycle Moon Phase: _____

Cycle Phase: _____ Cycle Season/Archetype: _____ Cycle Day: _____

Fertile: ✿ ✿ ✿ ✿ ✿ ○  PMS/Cramps: ✯ ✯ ✯ ✯ ✯  Flow: ◊ ◊ ◊ ◊ ◊

Hours of Sleep: _____ Mood: _____

Present Statement: _____

Transformation Theme: _____

Medicines: _____

I Feel in my Body: _____

Environment/Notes: _____

*I Feel Emotionally:* _____

*I Think–Beliefs/Stories/Awarenesses:* _____

*I Am Weaving:* _____

*I Intuit/Desire:* _____

# Connect with Srimati

If you would like to further connect regarding any aspect of this journal, you can connect with Srimati online at:

www.srimatiaryamoon.com

Made in the USA
Monee, IL
13 October 2021